VINO
BUSINESS

VINO BUSINESS

THE CLOUDY WORLD OF FRENCH WINE

ISABELLE SAPORTA

TRANSLATED BY KATE DEIMLING

Grove Press
New York

First published in France in 2014 by Éditions Albin Michel

First Grove Atlantic hardcover edition: November 2015
First Grove Atlantic paperback edition: November 2016

Published simultaneously in Canada
Printed in the United States of America

ISBN 978-0-8021-2570-5
eISBN 978-0-8021-9088-8

Grove Press
an imprint of Grove Atlantic
154 West 14th Street
New York, NY 10011

Distributed by Publishers Group West

groveatlantic.com

16 17 18 19 10 9 8 7 6 5 4 3 2 1

I am grateful to all the great or unrecognized winemakers who fight for their wine every day.

CONTENTS

Introduction   1

1   The Bordeaux Elite and the Fête de la Fleur   5

2   Louis Vuitton and Prada Make Wine   11

3   The Hidden Side of the System:
Blockbuster Wines   19

4   The Classification Scandal   29

5   Such a Nice Dictator   37

6   With a Bogus Authority, the INAO   47

7   And in the Middle, a Handful of Alchemists   55

8   That Hide a Dangerous Secret   65

9   Maintained by Curious Methods   75

10   Praised by an Enthusiastic Court   79

11   A Very Nice Carnival   87

12   Bordeaux Is Booming in China   95

13   Vino China   103

14 The Sharks Divide Up the Land   109
15 The Long March of the Pomerol Exiles   115
16 You Have to Think Bigger   123
17 The Helicopters of Good Taste   135
18 Little Arrangements Between Lords   141
19 Pesticide Victims   149
20 The One Who Said No   157
21 A Little Guy Among the Greats   167
22 Tribulations of a Bordeaux Winemaker in China 175
23 The CAP Jackpot   185
24 Fear, or the Reign of Modern Oenology   189
25 My Kingdom for a Chip   197
Afterword   203

Acknowledgments   205
Notes   207

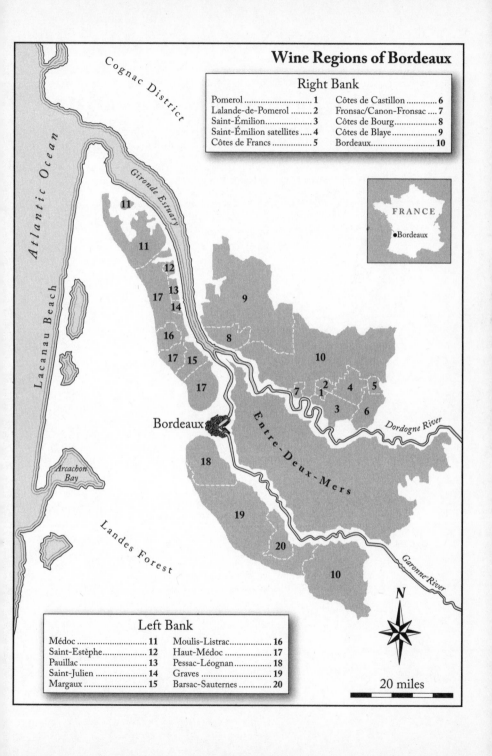

Wine Regions of Bordeaux

Right Bank

Pomerol 1	Côtes de Castillon 6
Lalande-de-Pomerol 2	Fronsac/Canon-Fronsac 7
Saint-Émilion.................... 3	Côtes de Bourg................. 8
Saint-Émilion satellites 4	Côtes de Blaye 9
Côtes de Francs 5	Bordeaux.......................... 10

FRANCE
•Bordeaux

Cognac District

Atlantic Ocean

Gironde Estuary

Lacanau Beach

Arcachon Bay

Landes Forest

Bordeaux

Entre-Deux-Mers

Dordogne River

Garonne River

N

20 miles

Left Bank

Médoc 11	Moulis-Listrac.................. 16
Saint-Estèphe................... 12	Haut-Médoc 17
Pauillac 13	Pessac-Léognan................ 18
Saint-Julien 14	Graves 19
Margaux 15	Barsac-Sauternes 20

VINO
BUSINESS

INTRODUCTION

In France, we have no shale gas, no gold mines, and no oil wells, but we have wine, including our famous Bordeaux, whose wines date back to our earliest history. The story of Bordeaux begins with the Roman Empire, when wine was already a coveted symbol of wealth praised by the greatest poets, such as Ausonius. And while Rome's decline led to a darker time for this region, the twelfth century and the marriage of Eleanor of Aquitaine to the future king of England, Henri II, led Bordeaux to glory—until the Hundred Years' War between France and England. Bordeaux then looked to Holland, then to still other markets, until its most recent conquest: China.

Bordeaux is divided into two distinct regions: its left bank, the Médoc, and its right bank, the Libournais. The Médoc's first classification was organized in 1855 by influential merchants and brokers who decided which wines were worthy of belonging to the holy of holies. The classification has remained almost unchanged since then—except that the terroirs covered by it have been greatly expanded. But who cares! The wine still sells just as well. Now that the estates have become huge, many have fallen into corporate hands.

As for the right bank, until recently it had remained in general more family owned. Its wines were not classified until a hundred years after the Médoc. The classification is revised every ten years in order to be fair and give new challengers a chance to succeed. This was an admirable intention on the part of the creators of the 1955 classification, but they didn't imagine that each new version of the classification would launch a merciless war with colossal sums of money at stake.

The bitter battles fought by the greatest estates to have their wines classified and to obtain the best terroirs resembles the most twisted machinations of *Dallas*. Modern-day J. R.s have entered the vineyards and made the prices of wine and land skyrocket. And just like the characters of *Dallas*, they don't shy away from using the dirtiest tricks to make this red gold soar.

This sector represents a lot of money: between €7 billion and €10 billion of export revenue (equivalent to $7.6 million to $10.8 million). And North America is one of our best customers, spending €2.4 billion yearly on our wine. Wine is second only to aeronautics in French exports and every year French journalists express the sales figures for wine in terms of fighter jets. The wine sector currently represents 157 jets, and we have a lot less trouble selling our fine wines than our planes.

So France is a wine power, and Bordeaux is a jewel that is especially popular abroad. Americans have developed a special relationship to it. It's thanks to an American that Bordeaux became an international name. Yet this relatively unknown young man received a cool reception when he first arrived in the Bordeaux region back in 1982. The local château owners looked at him with haughty contempt and had to be persuaded to open their doors. Almost no one at the time could have guessed that this American whom they snubbed would become the Million-Dollar Nose, Robert Parker, the man whose hundred-point grading scale makes and destroys the global reputation of wines.

Bordeaux's golden age came about through the convergence of several factors: a strong dollar, a flourishing market, and wealthy golden boys who were looking for any chance to blow their money. Robert Parker gave them this chance by inventing a simple scoring system that even neophytes can master without getting bogged down in the arcane words *appellations d'origine contrôlée*, vintages, *domaines*, châteaux, *grands crus classés*, and *premiers grands crus*. Parker didn't just put Bordeaux in the spotlight; he also brought this prestigious appellation into American territory.

Bordeaux has now become a huge business, a subject of large-scale speculation, and a worldwide brand. But as with any great success story involving massive amounts of money, rapid growth has led to a host of new problems. In the Chinese market, Bordeaux winemakers must learn to navigate government interference and rampant counterfeiting. Back in France, wines are heavily treated with pesticides, leading to controversy and concern over health risks to workers and wine drinkers. Meanwhile, our wine-making elite jealously guards its position within the kingdom of France and doesn't hesitate to climb to the top by any means necessary. Say good-bye to the traditional family vineyard. Say hello to the world of Vino Business.

1

The Bordeaux Elite and the Fête de la Fleur

Security is tighter than at the French president's palace, with walkie-talkies, barricades, and bodyguards. After guests are asked to leave their cars, flocks of young women in white dresses shield them with umbrellas so they don't get soaked in the pouring rain while stepping to the golf carts that will take them to the château. The anticipation is at its peak. A black sedan makes its way through the crowd, the only car permitted to enter the courtyard. It comes to a stop, and French actress Carole Bouquet emerges, looking magnificent.

Welcome to the Fête de la Fleur, the highlight of the spring season for the crème de la crème of the world of Médoc and the other wines of Bordeaux's left bank. In 2013, this huge party thrown by the *Commanderie du Bontemps*, the self-proclaimed "wine brotherhood" of Bordeaux's left bank, took place on the last day of the big wine show Vinexpo in Saint-Julien-de-Beychevelle, at Château Lagrange, which is owned by the Japanese company Suntory, the alcohol and soft drink giant whose holdings include the Orangina Schweppes Group. It's a magical place, the sign of a time when big capital has invested in vineyards and businessmen have replaced winegrowers.

The Bordeaux wine industry has become adept at bringing VIPs on board and crafting a swanky image. In thirty years, this very private world has undergone a sea change. The important wine figures of yesteryear have yielded to wealthy investors, traditional winegrowers have been pushed aside by CEOs, and old vineyard owners have been replaced by movie stars. In just three decades, the business has radically changed in scope. Big capital has invaded the vineyards, bringing its marketing managers and PR apparatus. And the guilds, those old bastions of the Bordeaux bourgeoisie where the local officials used to love to get together, now hold glamorous celebrations that resemble Hollywood premieres.

In the multimillion-euro splendor of the Fête de la Fleur, with its chandeliers and gilded ceilings, deals are closed and reputations are forged. No self-respecting wine merchant or established winegrower would think of missing it. But it's not cheap. Members of the Commanderie du Bontemps, the so-called commanders, pay €5,000 for a table for ten. Despite this high price, they all jump at the chance to get a table and invite celebrities, important clients, and those to whom they owe a favor. These ten seats provide the opportunity to display not only your power but also your gratitude. Of course, the well-known wine critics are seated at the best tables, including Jean-Marc Quarin, a Bordeaux critic who simultaneously proclaims his integrity as he grabs a spot at these elite shindigs. Or the American critic James Suckling, formerly of *Wine Spectator*, who describes himself as a California surfer who fell into wine by chance. Just a few years ago, he said that he loved Berlusconi and hated France and its pathetic soccer team. He also declared that Bordeaux was over.[1] A few tables away sits Michel Rolland, the man who invented the profession of wine consultant. You may remember him as the man of almost Mephistophelian power who was seen in the movie *Mondovino* commanding his driver with the same authority he exercises in the vineyard. The owners of the greatest estates are here too, such as Pierre Lurton, head of Cheval Blanc and Yquem. The most prestigious Bordeaux vineyards are all represented. The circle is large, but not too large—a handpicked elite.

In 2013, there were only fifteen hundred tickets and competition to obtain them was fierce. The day before, people were still trying to wangle a ticket. "I heard that such and such château still has one available," one local whispered to me. "I'm going to call them!" People worm their way in—or at least they try. After all, your presence may not be noticed, but your absence will be.

That was the experience of Bernard Pujol, head of the wine purveyor Bordeaux Vins Sélection. He is handicapped from a serious boating accident. As soon as he received the announcement, he rushed to reserve a table, but apparently he was not deemed prestigious or successful enough, for he was rejected. Two of his most important clients, SAQ (the Société des alcools du Québec) and the international

French-owned supermarket chain Auchan, had asked for seats at his table. Aggrieved and embarrassed at losing face, he decided to sue the head of the Commanderie du Bontemps in Bordeaux civil court. "I look like a clown in front of my clients, like somebody with no influence, and that's bad for business."[2] He's seeking €500,000 in damages. But he's willing to settle if the Commanderie will hear his arguments. "They'll listen. You just have to put enough pressure on them," he told me, with a smile.[3]

This elite world may look civilized and discreet. But being excluded from it can mean financial ruin. The day of the event, the organizers made sure that no interlopers managed to crash the party, which was indeed a splendid one. You have to be made of strong stuff to survive being left out of this charming little clique. A few rebels make a point of boycotting these high-class affairs. One of them is the world-renowned wine consultant Stéphane Derenoncourt. Every year he thumbs his nose at the Bordeaux elite by throwing an anti–Fête de la Fleur with the cellar masters—the laborers whose hard work is behind the production of fine wines. He likes to call it the beggars' ball. Derenoncourt hasn't forgotten his roots. After a troubled childhood in northern France, he moved to the Bordeaux region and started at the bottom of the ladder as a laborer in the fields. In twenty years, he worked his way up from vineyard worker to internationally renowned wine consultant. Refusing to attend the Fête de la Fleur is his way of rejecting the privileged classes of Bordeaux, who wanted nothing to do with him when he was just a nobody.

That evening, as soon as guest of honor Carole Bouquet had gotten out of her car, the Commanderie began to pay her its respects. She was entitled to this privilege not just as a famous actress, but also as a winemaker. She has a vineyard on the Sicilian island of Pantelleria. In Michel Rolland's opinion, her wine is not even worth carrying back to the mainland—perhaps a harsh assessment, but who cares? A gorgeous winemaker–actress is the perfect image. Two other actresses—Bond girl Michelle Yeoh and Karl Lagerfeld's muse Anna Mouglalis—were also wearing the Commanderie's traditional wine-colored robes. In addition to famous actresses, as well as the Japanese ambassador, there were the big clients, especially Chinese wine importers—everyone who makes the Bordeaux market what it is today, that is to say, extremely speculative. The Fête de la Fleur is for thanking and honoring those who make Bordeaux thrive, and this exceptional wine industry has made its living from China ever since that country developed a thirst for red wine.

A few days before, under clearer skies, the Jurade de Saint-Émilion held its own event on the right bank. Of course, it wasn't quite as nice, since the right bank doesn't have as much money as the Médoc. At least that's what the local gossips say (and there are many of them). But Hubert de Boüard, president of the Jurade and the owner of one of the biggest *crus classés*, Château Angélus, maintains that Saint-Émilion represents history, knowledge, and culture, while Médoc is for shopkeepers, even nouveaux riches. Be that as it may, Saint-Émilion couldn't have gotten Michelle Yeoh or Anna Mouglalis, not to mention Carole Bouquet.

The only actor who deigned to make the trip is Stéphane Henon, who plays a police officer on the French soap opera *Plus belle la vie*. But Chinese and American investors also had a place of honor in the picturesque village of Saint-Émilion, which is a UNESCO World Heritage site. As at the Fête de la Fleur, the highest honors go to those who make deals, not wine.

There was not an empty seat at the Fête de la Fleur, but at the Jurade de Saint-Émilion some tables were sparsely filled. Two major figures in the world of fine wine refused to attend: Pierre Lurton of Cheval Blanc and Alain Vauthier of Ausone. Their wines were the first ever to be classified as Saint-Émilion *premiers grands crus* but, for them, it would have been a disgrace to attend this flashy ceremony put on by the man they've nicknamed Hubertus Magnus or don Hubert de Saint-Émilion. It is this man, Hubert de Boüard de Laforest, who is responsible for the Saint-Émilion classification scandal.

Welcome to the private world of the *grands crus classés*, a.k.a. Vino Business, a kingdom that can be more cutthroat than Wall Street.

2

LOUIS VUITTON AND
PRADA MAKE WINE

He's not very tall, and he proudly displays the round belly of a bon vivant who enjoys the pleasures of the table. Two large wrinkles extend diagonally from his forehead, looking to all the world like devil's horns. His eyes sparkle, but they're also piercing. This jovial businessman with the sharp eyes, the man who punctuates all his sentences with a booming laugh even before they're finished, is Michel Rolland. The wine-making king of kings. The man who has spread the wine gospel to every corner of the world. But this savvy businessman, this modern shark of the wine industry, becomes wistful when he talks about his properties,[1] especially the family estate in Pomerol, Bon Pasteur, which he had to sell to satisfy the monetary desires of his lawyer brother.

Like many before him, he was caught up in the financial spiral that's taken hold of vineyards these last few years. The price of land has skyrocketed, whetting the appetites of all the heirs to these great dynasties.

"Why was Cheval Blanc sold, why was Pavie sold, why is everything being sold?"[2] asks Rolland, irritated. It's of course because the land is such a gold mine that the brother or sister who has left the family wine-making business behind won't agree to wait a long time before cashing in. "We try to get as much money as possible from the property to save it, but the profits are nothing compared to what the land is worth! It's only human that each person wants a piece of the pie."[3] And, at age seventy, Rolland's brother decided to get his.

All over Bordeaux, in a painful process, the current winemakers' siblings are now claiming their right to the riches within their grasp. When land reaches astronomical prices, it is indeed hard to rein in a family's dreams of instant wealth. A press attaché who knows Bordeaux well explained to me: "Just think of the brother or sister who didn't take up wine making and knows perfectly well that they're sitting on a colossal fortune that they can't touch! There's no way they'd accept this!" Not to mention the estate taxes, which reduce the chances that land will stay in the family even further. How can the heirs get access to that much cash when the money is all in the land?

Michel Rolland, like many others before him, had to resign himself to selling most of his estates—the very ones that made his reputation and his success—to a real estate conglomerate, Hong Kong's Goldin Group.

Rolland knows Goldin well because he was already a consultant for Sloan Estate in California, which it owns. The sale price was not released, but it must have been very high. People in the Bordeaux wine community believed it was on the order of €15 million. For that kind of money, you reluctantly give up the family estate. The one that belonged to your grandfather, a landowning Pomerol farmer. The one where your parents were wed in 1942. You forget the little stone bench that had been kept until then, a souvenir of all those old memories that make a family's history. "I can't let myself be melancholy. I don't have the means. It's fantastic to get to keep your estate. But when you can't, you have to stop being emotional."[4]

These small family tragedies play out every day in French wine country. Why is there such a crazy spike in land prices? Because big companies, afraid of stock market fluctuations and real estate speculation, decided to invest in land, creating a bubble. But big money hasn't invested everywhere; they've focused on the most prestigious appellations. Prices in Pomerol in 1993 were on average €292,000 per hectare and reached a peak of €2.35 million per hectare in 2012.[5] In Saint-Émilion, the increase is also staggering: €120,000 in 1993 versus €1.1 million today. Over twenty years, with the massive influx of money into renowned terroirs, prices have gone up almost by a factor of ten. And while this upward movement began in 2002 (when the Internet bubble burst), it became even stronger in 2008 during the financial crisis, with Pomerol passing the €1.7 million per hectare.

At the same time, in lesser-known appellations, such as Côtes de Castillon, despite its location right next to Saint-Émilion, prices have stagnated for twenty years: €16,100 per hectare in 1993, €21,000 today. In fact, prices are half what they were at their peak in 2002, when this magnificent land reached the modest record of €56,400 per hectare. At that time, investors thought they had found a new gold mine in this special place near the wonderful terroir of Saint-Émilion. They quickly dropped the idea, and the appellation along with it. "In Côtes de Castillon, prices are very attractive and yet no one wants to buy. But as soon as you're in Pomerol, everything sells for insane prices. Wine making is really a two-tier system,"[6] sighs Alain Vauthier, owner of the legendary vineyard Ausone, located in Saint-Émilion. While you could hardly call Côtes de Castillon disadvantaged, wines made there are sold at very inexpensive prices, its appellation is practically unknown, and its land will never be speculated on. But in the "rich man's" area, the situation is exactly the opposite.

But all is for the best in the best of all possible worlds—if you're well-off. Among the top fifty wealthiest vineyard owners, according to the magazine *Challenges*,[7] are names that the French public already knows for their colossal fortunes in other areas. Number one, as always, is LVMH chairman and CEO Bernard Arnault, whose vineyards are worth €1.5 billion and include treasures like Yquem and Cheval Blanc as well as a veritable empire in the Champagne region (Krug, Veuve Clicquot, Dom Pérignon—all told, some 1,717 hectares of Champagne grapes). His rival François Pinault, the majority shareholder of French luxury goods company Kering, whose subsidiaries include Alexander McQueen and Gucci, is in fifth place with vineyards worth €700 million, including the prestigious Château Latour. Also on the list: wine businessman Bernard Magrez (€525 million), Michel

Reybier, founder of the food company Justin Bridou (€450 million), engineering and communication magnates Martin and Olivier Bouygues (€250 million), Chanel owner Alain Wertheimer (€235 million), the Dassault family, famous for their aviation companies (€150 million), etc.

Land has three major advantages. First of all, it's a relatively stable investment compared to the wild fluctuations of the stock market. Moreover, land has tax advantages that allow the super wealthy to avoid part of the wealth tax (in France, a special tax applies to assets above a certain threshold, which is currently set at €1.3 million). Some of the capital gains from the successful companies these people own can be shifted to vineyards, which can tend to lose money or require large investments in infrastructure. Finally, vineyards offer all these businessmen a "passport to nobility."[8] "When a guy who makes bolts goes to fancy dinner parties, he's not very sexy, but if he takes out a card that says he's a winemaker with a château in Bordeaux or Burgundy or somewhere, all of a sudden people start to look at him differently,"[9] laughs winemaker Stéphane Derenoncourt.

These wealthy businessmen now have competition from institutional investors—banks, insurance companies, mutual funds—that have also gotten into wine to avoid stock market fluctuations, which, ironically enough, they often have a hand in causing. Château Lascombes in Margaux is said to have been sold for almost €200 million in 2011 to the insurance company MACSF.[10] Another insurance company, AGR2 La Mondiale, is said to have spent about €35 million[11] in Saint-Émilion to purchase Soutard, the Ligneris family estate. It's a colossal windfall, but the former manager François des Ligneris still misses his wonderful estate. According to the *Revue du Vin de France*, banks and insurance companies own 2,400 hectares (5,930 acres) of vineyards estimated at €1.4 billion, primarily in Bordeaux.[12]

And the newest arrivals in Bordeaux wine country? Chinese investors have bought about fifty châteaux in the last four years or about a thousand hectares of vineyards. "It's all very simple: if they buy so much wine and so many estates, it's because they have the money,"[13] says Rolland, who is surprised to see such an outcry in Bordeaux against Asian buyers when there was no criticism of the arrival of the institutional investors. "This is all just business. And it's quite good business,"[14] jokes the winemaker, a greedy look in his eye. "We should be glad that Bordeaux is still attracting big investors and the Chinese; if it stops happening, *then* we should be worried."

Dominique Techer doesn't share this enthusiasm. It should be mentioned that he's unusual for a Bordeaux wine-grower. A believer in organic produce, he started a vegetable garden on part of his land ("After all, this is the countryside!"),[15] while his neighbors have grapevines growing all the way to the road. "On the Pomerol plateau, there must be two or three wine-making families tops who are still around. We're the last of the Mohicans; soon people will come stare at us like curiosities. We're surrounded by pension funds, banks, insurance companies, and now the Chinese . . . The Chinese buy like any other investor. Five years ago, they bought wine. Today, they buy the estates."[16]

"Prices are spiraling out of control," admits Jean-Luc Thunevin. He's a Frenchman born in Algeria, where his parents raised pigs, and nothing in his background would have augured a future career in wine. After working as a woodcutter, he almost became a psychiatric nurse before changing directions and going into banking. "I started off in Saint-Émilion selling neon jewelry. Then, plot by plot, hectare after hectare, I created my Valandraud wine [called after his wife's maiden name]."[17] The wine has become legendary, but Thunevin's success story would be practically impossible to repeat today. The land in Saint-Émilion that he financed entirely for 1.5 million francs per hectare in 1999 is worth between €3 million and €4 million per hectare today.

On the Pomerol plateau, it's the same story: buyers snap up land at €3 million per hectare. "As soon as there's the least little bit of land for sale, there are fifty vultures diving onto it,"[18] according to Dominique Techer.

"It's the system that makes this happen," Jean-Luc Thunevin told me at another time. "Each time a plot sells, another winegrower leaves. And the more investors there are, the more expensive the land will be."[19]

"Average but good quality vineyards will disappear or belong to big companies. It's inevitable. No family will be able to keep hold of its estate,"[20] as Rolland put it.

Land is becoming more and more expensive, and super-wealthy vineyard owners will be tempted to make colossal investments, not only because there are tax advantages, but also because, as Stéphane Derenoncourt points out, they think of wine as a leisure pursuit and they're ready to sink millions of euros into their passion.[21] And because these are shrewd businessmen, not dreamers, of course their gambles will pay off. So their wines become brands sold at astronomical prices. With millions upon millions, they're creating the Louis Vuitton and Prada of wine.

So, through the magic of a speculative real estate bubble, French land that only the richest can afford to buy will produce great wines that the French won't be able to purchase. This is the state of our beloved wine-making tradition. Does it really have to be this way?

3

The Hidden Side
of the System:
Blockbuster Wines

The wine cellar of the Hôtel de Paris in Monaco, run by
the great chef Alain Ducasse, contains 350,000 bottles of
wine. Of these, 200,000 are Bordeaux. In just a few years,
this stockpile has become a treasure trove worth tens of millions of euros. Owners of the very finest vineyards, including
Pierre Lurton, head of Cheval Blanc and consul to Monaco,
are here to celebrate the 150th anniversary of the Société des
Bains de Mer in high style. But in this festive and luxurious
atmosphere, one man's frankness is out of place. The cellar
master Gennaro Iorio doesn't mince words: "I've decided
to punish Bordeaux. As of 2010, I don't buy their wines anymore. The *grands crus* are much too expensive; they're purely
for speculators. These wines are produced for foreigners,
investors, and the Chinese market. They aren't made for
drinking, but for hoarding, to play the stock market. This
wine is no longer accessible to the French market! It's not
even accessible to luxury establishments like ours."[1]

Château Angélus co-owner Hubert de Boüard views Iorio's stand with contempt. He confidently denies that this gold mine is a mirage, that this speculative bubble that has made them all so rich and has kept us from drinking our finest wines will one day burst. "We've created wines with strong brands, like any luxury products. These brands cost money, and that's normal,"[2] he told me defensively.

Yes, but for how much longer? Large retailers are also tired of these permanently rising prices. Fabrice Matysiak buys about 7 percent of the wine produced by volume in Gironde for the Auchan supermarket chain. He predicts a price collapse. "For now, we don't buy fine Bordeaux wines anymore. They're much too expensive and none of our customers can spend that kind of money on a bottle of wine! Who, except for a few rich foreigners who aren't shopping at big-box stores, can afford to spend three hundred to a thousand euros for a *grand cru classé*?"[3]

Gérard Margeon, head sommelier for Groupe Alain Ducasse, has already noticed a backlash against Bordeaux. "The year 2013 was the first year when all these fine gentlemen came in person to knock on my door with their little refrigerated carts to show me their wine. They clearly know it's going badly."[4] This wine professional's logic is unassailable: "The prices they're offering us now are the same as the prices on our menus. So, every year, we eliminate types of Bordeaux. These wonderful wines now represent only ten percent of what we sell in our restaurants."[5] How could it be otherwise, even for a devoted wine lover? "We need to consider what we can still buy for a hundred euros," Margeon points out. "In Burgundy, you get a *grand cru*. In Bordeaux, you get one-fifth of a *très grand cru*."[6]

Even though Stéphane Derenoncourt works for all these prestigious estates, he shares this feeling. For him, there are about fifteen overvalued labels that, despite their quality, don't have much to do with wine anymore. He sees them as purely speculative in their value. And he rages against the arrogance of a few *grands crus* that hide all the variety of Bordeaux—all the small wine producers who are struggling to sell their wines at decent prices. All these farmers will end up disappearing as long as the revenue from their wines is nothing next to what their land is now worth. Little by little, wine country thus seems condemned to gentrification. Just as the underprivileged have been excluded from our urban centers, soon small farmers will be banished from their own land. Big investors will control everything. Small wines will disappear and flashy brands will emerge—until the system becomes saturated and the investors flee.

We're not there yet. Quite the opposite—prices have spiked. The results are clear: in just a few years, fine French wines have shed their old-fashioned charm and become true luxury products. If there's one thing these big investors know how to do, it's to turn lead into gold and wine into brands. Until they came in, France was proud to display on its wine labels the *appellations d'origine contrôlée* (AOC): Saint-Émilion, Pomerol, Pommard, Volnay, Puligny-Montrachet, etc. These names epitomized the prestigious French terroirs where the finest wines have been produced through the ages.

But the businessmen realized that the quaint, old-fashioned charm of AOCs was much too complicated to market and that they had to retreat behind symbols that were more readable and easy to understand. Everyone recognizes the success of the brands Cheval Blanc (owned by LVMH and Albert Frère) and Yquem (LVMH), and, more importantly, everyone wants them. The appellation, which used to be a marker of quality, has been replaced by the brands of the individual châteaux.

Sommelier Gérard Margeon is very critical of the purchase of estates by rich financiers: "These people don't have the sensitivity to make wine and it shows in their vintages. This isn't their natural job. In Provence or in Bordeaux, I've seen what they do: they buy a beautiful house, they open the door, and say, 'Oh, there's a vineyard!' And then they think, 'Hey, what if I become a farmer?'"[7] And he deals a final blow: "I always ask myself what the message hidden behind the label is. These people only talk about themselves and their brand, not about the wine at all."[8]

But in French vineyards, the investors' ways have caught on, and the châteaux that haven't yet fallen into their hands are also taking the same approach. They need a name that sounds right and a symbol that's eye-catching. Hubert de Boüard has figured this out. The name of his wine, Angélus, "sounds good to English speakers, to the Chinese, to everyone!"[9] And even if some Asian buyers may have a hard time pronouncing the French, they recognize the bell on the label. Hubert is pleased with this bell, which is for "making money in every corner of the world."[10] In China—now the biggest market for Bordeaux wines—bells symbolize prosperity. "When they made their label, the de Boüard family couldn't put their château on it. Because they only had a house, they would've looked like country bumpkins," smirks an old Saint-Émilion resident. "That's why they put the bell on."[11] But who cares about the reason for the bell, for the ups and downs of history? When you can make use of symbolism and have marketing are on your side, why not go for it?

Create buzz, get your name out there, make noise, do something big, or perish. That's the false dilemma in which many players in this environment are trapped. In a few decades, the job of wine producer has radically changed. Here, as elsewhere in the world, if you can't tell a great story, the kind that brings tears to consumers' eyes—and journalists' eyes, too—then you're dead. As Stéphane Derenoncourt told me, "In the past, we asked winemakers to make good wine, and that was all. Today it's different. They have to make good wine, know how to talk about it, and know how to sell it. They have to be communicators, salespeople, winegrowers, and winemakers, all at the same time."[12]

So it's necessary not just to create a brand, but also to stay a step ahead, to remain at the forefront, and to stand out. Otherwise you don't exist.

Jean-Luc Thunevin, the winemaker born in Algeria who was once a woodcutter, is aware of these requirements more than anyone. He embraced the "bad boy" name that Robert Parker, the king of wine critics, is said to have given him. He didn't just appropriate it. He made it his symbol and trademark, putting an image of a black sheep on the wine he named Bad Boy. Bad Boy is classified as *Bordeaux Supérieur*, a step above standard Bordeaux, but not as prestigious as the regional appellations. Nevertheless, Thunevin is able to sell it at much higher prices than most Saint-Émilion. Although he struggled to sell it for €5 a bottle under the name Compassant, now it flies off the shelves at €15, just because it bears the famous black sheep. In Korea, one of his distributors even produced a tailor-made video for him.

And to give even more luster to his Saint-Émilion *grand cru*, Valandraud, he tried to bring the famous Chinese pianist Lang Lang on board. It was a smart choice due to their similar backgrounds. Like Jean-Luc, Lang Lang started his career as a black sheep: he was a pariah for a while among the best classical musicians and dismissed by critics before finally being idolized. This microvintage of five thousand bottles was going to be priced even higher than Valandraud, for somewhere between €500 and €1,000. That's the price of great marketing. If this idea had come to fruition, it would have been a stroke of genius for Jean-Luc Thunevin: this wine might have let him conquer the Chinese market, which, so far, has not been interested in his *grand cru*. Alas, so far Lang Lang seems hesitant about the idea. Perhaps Valandraud isn't glamorous enough for the rock star of classical pianists.

As for Hubert de Boüard, he bet on James Bond. Angélus has become the favorite wine of secret agents ever since it appeared for seven long seconds in *Casino Royale*—a sweet deal to be in a big-budget production distributed worldwide.

Yet he swears that no monies were paid and that he owes this fabulous gift only to his friendship with the producer's family and the many cases of wine he sent them. Hard to believe when it costs €15,000 for product placement for a few seconds in a French film.

Producing wine means producing PR. And having your product featured in this way is a weapon like any other to get your name out there.

This elite society figured out that it's not enough to have the wine; you also need to have the setting. A château is good, but you need more than that. You also need to make the whole production of *grand crus* glamorous—to make even the utility room worthy of a photo shoot. In a nutshell, wine making is all about image. These rich investors have all thrown themselves into a race for fabulous wineries. Gone are the old-fashioned cellars where the winemaker worked with a Gitane hanging from his lips. Now great architects from the world over charge obscene amounts to build these buildings where the precious nectar is made. In French wine country, as in Rioja in Spain or Napa Valley in California, the wealthy battle to see who can have the most gigantic winery built by the most famous architect.

Clément Fayat, the public works magnate, hired renowned French architect Jean Nouvel, for example. A juicy detail: his estate, La Dominique, is just a stone's throw away from the prestigious Cheval Blanc. Fayat is very unhappy that his wine is not recognized for what he sees as its true value, and he's terribly jealous of Cheval Blanc. Bernard Arnault, owner of Cheval Blanc, employed the services of onetime Pritzker Prize winner Christian de Portzamparc.[13] His winery is shaped like a wave floating over the vineyard, but its simplicity competes with La Dominique's gleaming deep-red barge—the color of fine wine—and its changing shades. Decorated with colored mirrors, Jean Nouvel's building reflects the countryside around it (including Cheval Blanc) upside down. Intensely irritated by this nearby structure, Pierre Lurton, the very elegant manager of Cheval Blanc, tells anyone who will listen that his competitor's building is so ugly that all the visitors think it's the production building of LVMH's wine! To hide the horror of what he calls the microwave, he has planted gigantic trees that block La Dominique's views of the countryside. This petty neighborly squabble is just a game that the local stars enjoy. They throw around millions of euros to inflict small humiliations and play tricks on one another.

There are dozens of examples. For instance, Faugères, owned by Silvio Denz (owner of Lalique), signed up Swiss architect Mario Botta to build a concrete cathedral in the middle of the grapevines. The real estate company Pichet, which recently bought the Château Les Carmes Haut-Brion in Pessac-Léognan for the trifling sum of €18 million, hired renowned nightclub decorator Philippe Starck.

In such surroundings, fine wines truly become luxury products. No more exceptional bottles for less than three figures. You're either a brand that gets respect or you're not.

"Our finest wines are no longer accessible! Who today can spend a thousand euros on a bottle of wine, even splitting it with three others? It's not as if there's gold inside!"[14]

exclaims Dominique Techer, a rebellious farmer hanging on to his land on the prestigious Pomerol plateau. In fact, these wines aren't purchased for drinking. They're the external sign of wealth that golden boys and apparatchiks buy to show off their success. Worst-case scenario: they'll be kept in cellars. Best-case scenario: they'll be swilled down to thrill an audience.

In Ürümqi, in northwestern China, a bigwig at an international Chinese company, who showed obvious signs of a big hangover, publicly boasted of downing €160,000 of fine wine in one week "*gan bei*," meaning at one go. All that effort, all those millions of euros invested, sequins and glitter put on, to end up like a cheap shot of vodka!

But there are still more surprises in store, for this enchanted kingdom is based at its very foundation on an outrageous system.

4

THE CLASSIFICATION
SCANDAL

On October 24, 2012, a leaden sky hangs low over the pretty village of Saint-Émilion. "What a shame to have such bad weather for a fancy celebration," smirk all those who aren't invited. The whole village is talking about the event. Today, Hubert de Boüard is having the bells of Angélus blessed—a fitting celebration of his wine's reaching the top ranking: *premier grand cru classé A*.

Bursting with impatience to flaunt his success before wine world insiders, Hubert sent out invitations even though the massive €7 million renovation of his winery is far from complete. So what? The outlines of the new structure are there, designed by Jean-Pierre Errath, an architect with a degree in restoring historical buildings who made his reputation by redesigning Pétrus's buildings in Pomerol. In seeking legitimacy, Angélus couldn't have asked for a better connection, even if only an aesthetic one.

Amid the rubble and construction equipment a platform has been set up where soprano Sharon Coste will sing Schubert's *Ave Maria*. The unfortunate archbishop of Bordeaux, Monsignor Ricard, is in a cherry picker suspended fifty feet above the void so that he can consecrate the two bells (named Émilion and Angélus). As if to show the peasants that this wine is indeed blessed by the gods, the sun comes out as the ceremony begins, making the gilded bells gleam. These bells play not only the traditional chimes for the Angélus prayer, but also over one hundred national anthems, "so we can welcome our big clients in a personalized way. We've got all the anthems: the US, China, the UK, but also Iceland, the Philippines, Kazakhstan, Monaco, and the Vatican, in case Francis ever comes to see us!"[1] rejoices Laurent Benoit, the estate employee who handles the remote control, and plays the bells with delight. This display is ostentatious and grotesque, grandiose and ridiculous—and certainly kitschy—and the wine merchants and journalists in the audience are definitely blown away. The lord of Saint-Émilion has pulled it off. But not everyone is impressed. "I used to have a warm place in my heart for the Saint-Émilion classification; it felt connected to the land and to farmers. It was the worth of the terroirs that determined the classification. There were a few mistakes but that was really what it was about,"[2] says Stéphane Derenoncourt.

In reality, there's not just one but two beauty contests (so to speak) in Bordeaux. People always contrast the terroir-based classification of Saint-Émilion from 1955 with the more commercial classification of Médoc, which was established by wine merchants and brokers a century earlier and has hardly changed since then.[3] "Except for the fact that the estates that were classified in the past were ten hectares and now they're one hundred hectares, but have kept the same ranking," specifies Stéphane Derenoncourt. Which means that many acres of vineyards have thus surreptitiously reached great heights even though they were previously deemed unworthy of this ranking. The owners have raked it in, buying lands that are worth millions now that they're classified. Consumers are paying hundreds of euros for these wines that supposedly are from the best terroirs. To put it succinctly, in Médoc brands had been classified but Saint-Émilion had kept its authenticity.

The best proof of the open mind of the Saint-Émilion classification was the fact that the small village's winemakers had to reapply for their ranking every ten years so that they wouldn't rest on their laurels and obvious injustices could be corrected. "This classification is one of the last remainders of Gaullism, with a true meritocracy,"[4] adds Hubert de Boüard, struck by a sudden lyricism. But this is far from certain. With so much money at stake, every new version of the classification has launched a civil war. The last episode was especially bloody.

To understand what happened, you have to consider the context of the time. "In 2006, a lot of people didn't like the classification," explains a wine producer who knows the local customs well and owns one of the greatest estates in the world. "Hubert de Boüard wasn't a *premier grand cru classé A*. Jean-François Quenin, current president of the

Saint-Émilion Wine Council [the wine syndicate], wasn't classified. So there were a lot of people in high places who wanted the classification to collapse, and it did."

In 2008 Hubert stepped down as president of the Saint-Émilion Wine Council, a position he had held since 1999. That would have been a bit too much. But his right-hand man, Jean-François Quenin, succeeded him. The winemakers find it funny to watch Quenin constantly look to Hubert de Boüard in meetings to see whether he approves or disapproves of something before making a decision. And Hubert's ingenuity seems to know no bounds. Instead of calling his wine l'Angélus in French, he removed the article and named it simply Angélus, so it could be the very first on the list of *premiers crus classés* in alphabetical order.

The changes made to the points system for the *classement* of the wines of Saint-Émilion in 2012 were far reaching. The monumental architecture constructed in the middle of the vineyard would now get a winemaker good marks. The classification criteria would also wisely allot some points for the size of the visitors' parking lot that accompanied it so that all the peasants could come admire a winemaker's beautiful building. Finally, there is the seminar room: a jackpot for former industry leaders who can get their connections to rent this heavenly location is worth a few extra points.

Wine lovers will be thrilled to learn that when they drink a glass of a *grand cru classé* that costs €500 a bottle, they're also tasting a bit of its parking lot and event space. On the contrary, Ausone, the Romanée-Conti of Saint-Émilion, is located at the top of a steep road where buses can't go. It not only lacks a lecture room but also had the bad taste to keep its historical cellar building—and so was penalized. The stone cellars of Ausone, rich with five centuries of history, paled in comparison to grandiose wineries by architects Christian de Portzamparc or Mario Botta: "Outdated, no indirect lighting," criticized the commission. It's too much, especially when you consider that Ausone's kind of cellar is, according to Stéphane Derenoncourt, "a wine-making cathedral." That may be, but it's clearly not spectacular enough for Hubert's taste.

The billionaires who've invested in wine may be willing to bend themselves to the duty of wine tourism, but they're reluctant to become tour guides for their own châteaux. But no worries: the classification standards penalize winemakers who want to lead tours themselves. The manager of Château Croque-Michotte, Pierre Carle, discovered this the hard way. The commission held it against him that his daughter welcomed visitors. When he complained that this was ridiculous, the commission asked him to provide a copy of her work contract as well as her degrees. A winemaker who is involved in his château is automatically under suspicion!

The classification doesn't like environmentalism either. Ausone's vineyards were considered to be "badly managed" by the inspection office. And Croque-Michotte, which has been organic since 1999, got a very mediocre grade for environmental measures. Why? What could be more environmental than this approach?

"This classification is the essence of bad faith," rails a Saint-Émilion winemaker who prefers to remain anonymous because the retaliatory measures against those who complain are so harsh. "They focus attention on insignificant things; they create a mythology to avoid all the sensitive topics: pesticide residue, soils that are chemically overtreated. In this classification, they use and abuse the same methods as for producing brands."

The new Saint-Émilion classification standards rate the cellar, the renovations, the parking lot, and the seminar rooms, but where does the taste come in? After all, that's the only thing a wine lover who's dropping lots of money on a *grand cru classé* is interested in, right?

Well, taste counts for only 50 percent of the grade for *grands crus classés* and for only 30 percent for *premiers grands crus*. This means that the more prestigious a wine is—the more it costs, and the better it's supposed to be—the less its taste counts in the classification. Simply put, for the *premiers crus classés*—the Rolls-Royce of French wines, which cost between €30 and €1,000 a bottle—reputation is worth more points than taste: 35 percent versus 30 percent.

With these criteria created ad hoc to satisfy a very few, a wine could become a *premier grand cru classé* with a tasting grade of 6.67 out of 20.

"There's no more classification based on terroir anymore. It's all just pure marketing. If you have a visitors' parking lot, you get two more points; if the hostess is hot, you get two more. And if you're in James Bond, that's even better! Everything shiny gets you points. It's totally ridiculous. It has nothing to do with the world of wine. But that's how it is,"[5] says wine expert Stéphane Derenoncourt, with sarcasm and regret.

All these criticisms deeply wound Christian Paly, the president of the INAO's National Committee for Wines, which is the bogus authority on vineyards that determines the classification. Paly believes that this institution has shown "incredible courage and seriousness" in developing this fabulous competition. "When the classification was suspended in 2006, the INAO could have acted like Pontius Pilate and washed its hands of it at the risk of rejecting its history. That wasn't our aim. We decided, on the contrary, to take up our responsibilities and to build the methodology of the classification as solidly as possible, with great seriousness and impartiality."[6]

Paly also sees himself as acting democratically. "The rules of this association are simple: when we decree a way of doing things, we always do so only in accordance with the interests of all." According to him, this is the reason for the organization's longevity: "If, ever since 1935, the INAO had worked to defend the interests of individuals, it would've disappeared a long time ago."[7]

Authenticity has lost out, but it's a lucky break for Hubert de Boüard. His promotion in the classification of 2012 let him increase the price of Angélus by 23 percent while *grands crus classés* like Margaux or Mouton Rothschild lowered their prices by 33 percent for *en primeur* sales in 2012 (the sales of *grands crus* that take place every April offering young wines harvested in October), since the vintage was not as good as the previous year. Today the Boüard clan is worth about €280 million and has climbed to seventeenth place in the list of the biggest wine fortunes. That must be what the INAO means by defending the interests of all.

5

SUCH A NICE DICTATOR

That day, all Bordeaux was waiting for him. Saint-Émilion was abuzz about his arrival. He was there; that was for sure. But no one had seen him yet. They just knew that early Monday afternoon he would stop by the Right Bank Circle, and its creator Alain Raynaud was very proud that he would be paying them a visit. On Thursday, he would be at wine consultant Michel Rolland's. In between, it was unclear. He'd surely go see some big wine merchants and visit a handful of carefully selected winemakers. But which ones? Behind the scenes, everyone was busy trying to lure him into their web. The man who is awaited like the messiah is Robert Parker, the great critic who makes and unmakes wines' reputations. The man whose score of 100 is golden. Yet no one would have bet on this obscure American when he came to Bordeaux in the late seventies. Imagine. A Yankee talking about wine? Analyzing and grading it? It had to be a joke. There was really no reason for the cream of Bordeaux society to be worried, and in fact they thought the whole thing was rather funny.

But they underestimated him—a mistake they have (for the most part) corrected since then. For despite his naïve manner, the American was tenacious and hardworking and tasted wine with a seriousness few others had. He acquired a special claim to fame: when the entire wine jet set panned the '82 vintage, he sang its praises. Time proved him right.

"Success is a lot of work, some luck, and a little bit of talent," says Michel Rolland mockingly. "He did what no one else was able to do. If he's the best, it's not because he's never wrong; it's just that he's wrong less often."[1]

Consultant Michel Rolland can't get over how incredibly lucky it was that he agreed to meet with Parker on a July day in 1982. "If I'd been swamped with work, if he had come during harvest time, if I hadn't felt that mad urge to leave my [oenology] lab like always, I would've missed the chance of a lifetime!"[2] the winemaker jokes. Fortune must favor the bold, for Rolland opened doors for Parker at a time when all the Bordeaux gentry turned up its nose and refused to meet with this guy who came from nowhere. The two built their careers together. Rolland taught Parker the customs of Bordeaux, and Parker was Rolland's entry into the United States.

This is how Rolland became a required stop for the man they call the Million-Dollar Nose, an apt nickname given that his nose and palate are indeed insured for that amount. Wine merchants Jeffrey Davies and Archibald Johnston, the Union of Grands Crus (a select club of many of the great Bordeaux wines), and the Right Bank Circle are also required stops. And now that everyone knows the almost divine power of his scores over wine sales, it's no small privilege.

"Parker is just like the Michelin Guide. Get three stars, and you know your restaurant will be full. Two stars helps. But with one star, you'd better work harder. A bad grade from Parker is dreadful news for an estate, which will have a terrible time selling its wine," assures a Bordeaux wine merchant. He could have added that not being graded by Parker at all leads to an anonymity that often signals the death of *grands crus*. "You have to get him to come to you, otherwise you don't exist," says winegrower Jean-Luc Thunevin, who regrets not having lobbied the master enough when his vintage, Valandraud, received a lower score for 2012. So we can see why being tasted and appreciated by Parker is so very important—and why winemakers would do anything to be on his itinerary.

Another man, Alain Raynaud, has gotten a nice reputation and significant clientele by astutely using his close contact with the king of critics. Over the years, he's managed to transform this friendship into a golden opportunity. "However, things didn't begin for us very auspiciously; we didn't start off on the right foot,"[3] Raynaud remembers. The 1982 vintage of his family estate, the Château La Croix de Gay, had received a scathing 78 out of 100 from Parker with the comment: "Good picnic wine." "But that's how we became friends. He was partly right. I wrote to him to ask him to come back in two years. And I changed my wine to get his approval. I got ninety-four points. He said, 'You're the only Bordeaux winemaker I gave a bad score to who didn't write me an insulting letter.'"[4] This must have touched Parker's heart, because since then, when he is in the Bordeaux area, he always stops by one of the various clubs that Raynaud runs.

Raynaud masterfully maintains the legend of his friendship, offering elusive proof of his closeness to the master. Is Parker actually the godfather of his daughter? "Shameful gossip," according to Raynaud, who didn't exactly discourage this myth when he prominently displayed a photo of his daughter dressed in white, carried like the holy sacrament by Parker in one of his former properties, the Château Quinault l'Enclos, which the critic elevated to the esteemed rank of the Haut-Brion of the right bank. "That was just to remember Bob's visit,"[5] explains Raynaud, in mock anger. And he accuses those who spread this erroneous information of slander—for of course it wasn't important that Parker actually be the godfather of Raynaud's daughter, just that everyone think he is. Raynaud, who is just a little bit megalomaniacal, even put a gigantic fresco in his vat room. It's a vineyard scene depicting all the current great wine tasters: Michel Bettane, Michel Rolland, and, of course, Robert Parker. In the sky, floating above these men, wearing a toga—a toga!—and a laurel wreath: Alain Raynaud.

His enthusiasm has sometimes led him astray. In 2000, he was president of the Union of Grands Crus and, knowing Parker loved fine food, he decided to give him a preview of wines at a restaurant called L'Aubergade, in Puymirol. L'Aubergade didn't yet have three Michelin stars but was already known as one of the best places in the area. Thanks to Hanna Agostini, who used to work with Parker, we know that the meal was excellent and that everything was done so the critic would be well disposed to score the wines he was offered.[6] The result? Raynaud's vintage, Château Quinault, got a very good score. This chumminess greatly displeased the Bordeaux bourgeoisie and Raynaud left his position as president of the Union of Grands Crus. So what? Next, he started the Right Bank Circle, which didn't hurt business any.

In fact, only one thing keeps this little club alive; otherwise, it would be an empty shell. Three times a year, Parker is sure to be there. He tastes all the wines his friend wants to offer him. How does it work? Just between friends! "The Right Bank Circle organizes a tasting that lasts all day, we taste together, we grade, we comment,"[7] Raynaud says as he proudly describes this privileged situation where, seated across from the master, he is present at his tasting. This business works so well that this year Raynaud has decided to extend it to the left bank (the Médoc) and to create a big circle.

With this huge advantage, the "good Doctor Raynaud" (he is also a country doctor and his enemies have given him this nickname) roams all over the Bordeaux region offering his services. "The owners hire him just so they can give samples of their wine to Parker. And as easy as pie you've got a nice little business bringing bottles to God," says an outraged oenologist who prefers to remain anonymous. "It's not a bad investment for the winemaker," says Stéphane

Derenoncourt wryly. "Because if it works—though it doesn't always—the contract soon has added value. It costs less than an annual advertising campaign in a newspaper."[8] And the payoff is much greater, because no ad has the impact of 100 points from Robert Parker.

An ad hoc alliance has recently come about between Alain Raynaud and Hubert de Boüard, the classification man. One brings the score, the other the possibility of becoming one of the top *premiers crus* in the world. Both things sell wine.

For instance, Jean-François Quenin,[9] president of the Saint-Émilion wine syndicate, has this double guarantee. In any case, the two-pronged approach works great, as the consultants who can't offer these services have learned the hard way. Stéphane Derenoncourt was dropped by Villemaurine, a château that he had advised for years. "Justin Onclin, a Bordeaux wine merchant and owner of the château, came to see me in my office and he said, 'Listen, Stéphane, you don't have the network. The wine is good but we can't get Parker to taste it.'"[10] Good-bye, Derenoncourt.

Derenoncourt is not crazy, of course, so naturally he tried to bring Parker in. But although he asked several times, the master did not deign to come. The other consultants were able to dissuade him.

A score from Parker isn't important because it means the wine tastes good—at least, that's not the only reason—but because it all but guarantees sales. Winemakers and consultants are fighting to be on his itinerary, but so too are wine merchants, who want to get a sense of the scores before they're made public. Knowing what Parker likes before the scores are released means that you can buy up wines before they become very expensive, thanks to the powers of the great kingmaker. Those in the know have gradually developed a lucrative system around Parker's influence by second-guessing his tastes.

"Why do you think the brokers agree to play secretary for Parker? To bring him all these bottles? To set up all his appointments? Why do all these guys with oversized egos agree to be at his beck and call? It's because their reward for all these little services is being able to taste with him. Right behind him, the broker whispers, 'Hey, did you like that one, Bob?' And the brokers buy or set aside the wines that Parker enjoys,"[11] the critic Jean-Marc Quarin aptly speculates.

To sum it up, all Bordeaux wants to make money from Parker and his scores. Even his former collaborator Hanna Agostini was dazzled by the gold mine he represented. After a falling-out with Parker, she wrote a tell-all book about him called *Anatomie d'un Mythe*. She was Robert Parker's devoted and beloved translator; she also managed his schedule and itinerary. A key position when we know how important is to be on the great man's path. The young woman also set up a PR business and started offering her services.

"Hanna Agostini had a consulting company. She suggested I become her client to help with my communication and wine presentation. It was clear that as Parker's translator, she was offering us access to him. Of course, it was very expensive; she asked for large sums, but it was valuable. All her clients were rewarded," explains a wine producer who didn't yield to her advances.

In her book, Hanna Agostini defends herself against these accusations, arguing that she was only making the master's tastings more transparent and accessible and that all those who controlled Robert Parker and his schedule conspired to bring about her fall.[12]

Whatever the truth may be, this business between friends could have lasted if Hanna Agostini hadn't been collateral damage in a huge fraud case involving a Belgian company. This company found itself accused of serious malfeasance: using prohibited wine-making products, selling surplus wine under fake labels—all matters that Hanna Agostini had nothing to do with. Agostini had merely opened up her address book to this company. In particular, she introduced people at the Belgian company to winemaker Jean-Luc Thunevin, who creates garage wines: microvintages crafted with great care and sold for exorbitant prices. Jean-Luc Thunevin was unaware "that Hanna Agostini was billing for this 'introduction.'"[13] When you're Robert Parker's main collaborator, all your advice is exceedingly precious because it opens the gates of heaven. Parker later broke off the relationship.

Until recently, the only person who made relatively little money from his name was Robert Parker himself. But he decided to prepare a comfortable retirement by selling his magazine, *Wine Advocate*, for $15 million to a group of investors from Singapore. The wine-making gentry trembled when this sale was announced. But Parker assuaged their worries by promising that he personally would continue to cover Bordeaux wines. Bordeaux breathed a sigh of relief, but for how long? They all watch for signs of weakness in the great man: he's gained weight, he's out of breath, his back hurts. And everyone speculates about his possible successor. Some are betting the next Robert Parker will be Chinese. The market has always determined the star critics, and China has now surpassed the United States as the biggest Bordeaux market. But will a new Parker have that magic power to make prices climb, to make wines into objects of such great speculation? And the ability to direct the market as much?

Meanwhile, the Singaporeans also seem determined to make their colossal investment pay off. At the last Vinexpo, Bernard Pujol, who heads Bordeaux Vins Sélection, a wine distribution and export company that is also partially owned by Hubert de Boüard, created a prestigious case with five *grands crus* from the 2009 vintage that received 100 out of 100 points from Parker. Six hundred cases of Robert Parker Selection were going to be sold for around €2,000 each. This modest price also included a year's subscription to the *Wine Advocate* and a short film about the master's tasting method. The box was also going to be signed by the great man. But after the news sparked an outcry, management decided to pull back. They okayed the subscription and the video, but not the signature. As for Pujol, he feels that he paid for this lapse of taste (or stroke of genius) by being excluded from the Fête de la Fleur and banned by the Bordeaux gentry. People are cruel.

However, this first case of personalized wine will go down in history, for merchandise hasn't stopped thriving. Jean-Luc Thunevin, owner of the classified *premier grand cru* Valandraud, had a good laugh about it. "Whether you like the idea or not, it's genius! Parker is a golden brand! This group didn't come up with fifteen million dollars just to buy a magazine. You'll see. Soon there will be stickers with Parker's ratings, and we'll have to pay to put them on our bottles. And we'll all pay, even those who are outraged today. For the plain and simple reason that it sells wine!"[14] the winemaker says caustically.

The Bordeaux community can laugh all the way to the bank. Parker is the best business deal they've ever made.

6

WITH A BOGUS AUTHORITY, THE INAO

"It's a very small world, and we're all close together. You have to know the customs, the language, and the mistakes to avoid. Once you know the rules, you're protected,"[1] Jean-Luc Thunevin says ironically.

The system is maintained because everyone knows his place. No one can really get out of line for fear of toppling this magnificent structure. As we've seen, the wine world functions totally independently. The profession is perfectly capable of regulating itself, just in its own special way. The idea is to at least maintain the appearance of impartiality without losing control of your future. The best way to demonstrate your virtue while remaining in charge is to choose your own watchdog. "More like a lapdog," laughs Jean-Luc Thunevin. An authority that is supposed to ensure that the standards for fine wine are respected. That is how the INAO was created. Its full name reveals its mission: National Institute for Origin and Quality. An institute that despite all their angelic displays is in the hands of those who truly run this charming little world.

Winemakers are wonderful storytellers. They love to tell tales by the fire to warm their hearts, hurt by the trials and tribulations of the current system. But the INAO is even better. It's a fairy tale invented to convince us that this inner circle is regulated by strict rules and monitored by undisputed ethical authorities. The reality is quite different.

The organization was founded with the best of intentions. In fact, it was a bighearted initiative, spearheaded by a man named Joseph Capus. This man, now totally forgotten, was minister of agriculture under the Third Republic and a senator from the Gironde department. He created the *appellations d'origine contrôlée* and an organization to regulate them.[2] This framework was designed so the wine industry, which had been hit hard by phylloxera, a tiny insect that attacks grapevines, could rebuild. It was intended to honor our terroirs and stem the wine fraud that was becoming increasingly common. The standards guarantee authenticity because not only must wine be shown to come from the region it claims, but the grapes must be grown in historical terroirs, on certain soil and with certain grape varieties that can make the finest wines. Basically, appellations are the ideal framework for a country like France that is attached to its history, the authenticity of its products, and the variety of its terroirs. That's the legend, anyway.

Unfortunately, this is all just a nice story. You just have to take a look at history to see that wine has always been an uncontrollable troublemaker. Every time lawmakers have put forward measures to make the field more ethical, winemakers have stripped them of meaning. Anyone with political power has always backed down for fear of offending the winemakers. And the winemakers were always able to get their hands on the organizations that were supposed to monitor them.

Between 1905, when the law establishing the regional boundaries of the *appellations d'origine* came into effect and started the crackdown on fraud, and 1935, when the structures for monitoring these appellations were created, the wine lobby again and again stripped all laws of their effective power. The industry would make its own laws.

The National Committee of Appellations and its soon-to-be outgrowth, the INAO, is therefore the kind of thing that France is so good at. In some respects, it shows how a public function can be seized by a profession that has prospered for decades amid general indifference.

When Champagne winegrowers rebelled in 1911 to stop the government from sticking its nose into their business, Capus understood that winegrowers would only agree to be led by their own kind. And in one masterful power play, the profession secured the right to police itself. Since winegrowing was a matter for specialists, the winegrowers would take charge. They would establish the rules that suited them, fixing boundaries for their territories, choosing the grape varieties and the yields, and also wielding the power to give out penalties, which provided them with a kind of legal authority.

Capus thought the profession would not compromise itself because it would give leadership to an ethical elite.

This elite would be chosen from the wine syndicates of the appellations, without going through voting by the majority, "which is disorganized and impulsive."[3] This way of appointing leaders was the icing on the INAO cake. And today the system remains unchanged. Marc Parcé, a winemaker in Banyuls and a member of the INAO's famous National Committee for the original appellation, is astonished by how arbitrary the system is. "There are no rules for nominations; they simply select whom they want. But generally a wine syndicate member is chosen."[4] He describes the pressure from each appellation to have their men rise through the ranks so they can seize power. "It's funny, because when you enter this little group, you realize how incredibly proud people are to belong to this caste. Basically, the French have a very monarchical concept of the republic,"[5] says Parcé.

The burning question is: how could they be so naïve as to create a paragovernmental organization that is supposed to report to the Ministry of Agriculture but is really only accountable to private interests? The fox is in charge of the henhouse. We'd be tempted to say, to paraphrase Rousseau, "If there were a people of gods, they would certainly govern according to these rules. But such a perfect government is not suitable for men."[6]

And indeed people acted as if the members of the committees of this outlandish institution were a people of gods, immune to temptation. As if they would never try to protect their own interests, establish economic advantages, or penalize their local competitors. As if having the power to set the boundaries of appellation areas as prestigious and popular as Champagne or Pomerol didn't have any financial implications. As if the winegrowers in charge of these issues were under no pressures and had no concerns other than the public welfare. One must have amazing faith in human nature to think that putting this legislation in the hands of these men wouldn't result in an inglorious outcome.

In fact, in all the appellations in which there are obvious financial stakes at play, a self-proclaimed local elite has taken the reins of power, supervising the wine industry in a quasi-permanent conflict of interest. And, appearances notwithstanding, the last reform of this strange authority by one of its presidents, René Renou, changed nothing. They updated the machinery with some new parts, but the apparatus stayed in place.

"A few guys control French wine making from the INAO; they're like big feudal lords," regrets Jean-Michel Deiss, an Alsatian winegrower attached to his terroir. "There aren't any more medieval prisons today, but there are still people who are suffering."[7]

To seem closer to their base and more open to the problems of the "nobodies," a special INAO committee of winemakers got rid of their old boss, Yves Bénard, after his term ended. Bénard was an insider who was the longtime director of champagne at LVMH, a real Gallic leader with powerful connections and friends in finance. They replaced him with Christian Paly, president of the wine-making cooperative Tavel. In such circles, that makes him practically a beggar—the representative of needy winegrowers. But, no worries, he's an apparatchik—not least, he directs the Inter

Rhône syndicate, the powerful organization of Rhône valley wines—and was able to skillfully assume his new responsibilities, which clearly give him great satisfaction.

When Christian Paly meets with people at INAO headquarters—in an imposing office with slightly kitsch décor and flanked by his second-in-command, Marie-Lise Molinier—this stout little man with a ruddy complexion looks as if he stepped right out of an Honoré Daumier caricature. Ensconced in his armchair, he attempts to make his bearing worthy of his new status. His speech is pompous and affected. Unfortunately, he stumbles over his words and must turn to his faithful assistant to approve or correct him if necessary. After mangling "ersatz" and "luxuriate," he gets to work defending his organization using ever more poetic language. He wants everyone to know that "the INAO is a special case in French administrative law," as he told me enthusiastically. "It's the sole public institution of its kind because it brings together agriculture ministers, finance ministers, and the professionals."[8] That's for sure! Anyone who dares to worry about the inherent conflicts of interest or injustice in this organization is quickly rebuffed: "People can't just accuse us of everything and its opposite! How could I manage this organization if I had to permanently cut myself off from the professionals?"

No, of course the organization will never cut itself off from them. On the contrary, it will listen to them closely to try, as much as possible, to meet their expectations and to be helpful.

Hubert de Boüard, who is a member of both INAO's Regional Committee and its National Committee, has a ready answer for those who would take exception to his presence in these conference rooms: "Missing two consecutive meetings means risking being banned from INAO's National Committee."[9] So it's pure civic duty, as well as ethical and contractual obligation, so to speak, that led him to attend these decisive meetings. He had no choice but to attend! "People should stop this gossip!" Christian Paly, head of the wine committee of the INAO, says with annoyance. As president, didn't he ask all these good people to leave the room when the final version of the classification was decided? But actually, why did they bother to leave?

In Saint-Émilion, people are uneasy. When the conflict of interest is local, everyone can compete, but now the syndicate isn't likely to rebel, and the classification watchdog isn't either. Hubert de Boüard now holds all the cards and lets it be known. "For two years, Hubert has been approaching clients to become their winemaker and saying, 'Hire me and you'll be classified,'" explains a person who is knowledgeable about Saint-Émilion. Hubert doesn't see anything controversial: "All the consultants had a lot of wines promoted. Some even had more than I did, and yet they're not part of the INAO committee!"[10]

When Marc Parcé, who is also a member of INAO's National Committee, is asked about the Saint-Émilion classification, he becomes uncomfortable and wonders if "the deck wasn't stacked." Then he adds, seemingly reluctantly,

"It was already all decided. They showed up with the applications all wrapped up. We couldn't do anything."[11]

It would be malicious to intimate that this corroborating evidence is any kind of proof of his closeness to the inner workings of the INAO.

"That Hubert is certainly fearless!" laughs one of the bigwigs in this lovely region. But for how much longer?

7

AND IN THE MIDDLE,
A HANDFUL OF ALCHEMISTS

Coming back from China, he stops in Turkey, and then goes to the United States (Virginia and California) before heading to Lebanon. Two days in Bordeaux, then Hong Kong and South Africa. Jet lag in one direction, then jet lag in the other. This is the hectic life of the so-called jet-set winemakers. They aren't called winegrowers or wine producers anymore, for the simple reason that they never touch the ground. They fly from vineyard to vineyard, crisscrossing the globe like the Energizer Bunnies of modern oenology. From Ürümqi to Cape Town, with stops in Beirut and São Paulo, it's always the same big names who are in charge of the wines and keep the enchanted kingdom running.

A small elite is at the head of the hierarchy. They are the top of the food chain in this pitiless world where the smallest are crushed before they can even grow. For about fifteen years, they've been paid incredibly well because they are thought to have enormous power: the power of making your wines exist by creating a brand and ensuring good sales, at a high price, if possible.

Their job? To advise the owners on managing their vineyards and making their wine. Michel Rolland invented the profession one day when he was tired of being stuck in his oenology lab in Pomerol. Anything to stop going stir-crazy! Observing the devastating effects of productivist agriculture in Bordeaux vineyards, Rolland had the idea of selling his advice to the owners in the late seventies and early eighties. The time was right because even in this place of storied tradition people had gotten carried away overusing fertilizers and pesticides to produce huge volumes. The wines were too light, and the yields were too big. The harvesting machines had transformed the grapes "into a witch's brew with toads, mice, and snails."[1] It had to be cleaned up. Rolland waxes poetic about his great accomplishments. "No one will ever see what I saw. I cleared a jungle with a machete, and I was able to impose a standard of quality."[2] He tasted the grapes and required yields to be reduced. In a few decades, he gained a reputation as a wine-making magician. "If these winemakers emerged, it's because there was a lack of quality in the *grands crus*,"[3] explains another consultant, Jean-Luc Thunevin, who launched the so-called garage wines. He made his reputation by making high-quality microvintages, which he sold at very high prices. "That's how I emerged. What's the beauty of garage wine? Wines produced with no money, in garages, but which we applied ourselves to as if they were designer fashion."[4] He criticizes all the *grands crus* that vaunted their Bordeaux location but made low-quality wines for years. "Since the wine wasn't good and people in Bordeaux have always been full of hot air, they told the buyers that if it was bad it was because the wines were closed. They said they just had to wait, since the very best wine always improves with age!" remembers Jean-Luc Thunevin with a laugh. "Some Bordeaux *grands crus* didn't even deserve to be put in bottles," according to Hubert de Boüard. "These very fine wines had some very dark hours."[5]

The excesses of intensive agriculture brought this new kind of alchemist front and center, but when the big investors and stars arrived their profession really took off. The beautiful people didn't know anything about growing grapes, and they needed excellent technicians, a great network, and good contacts to make their way in this opaque world. That's what the winemakers gave them. "Don't ever forget that all wine communications and consulting were built, grew, and thrived thanks to them," as one of the best press agents in the field sums it up. These rich newcomers had to learn not just to make wine but also, most of all, to sell it. "With them, we learned to create brands."

"We don't just bring them skill; we bring them a network. We introduce them to the wine merchants who count in Bordeaux, as well as the most powerful French and international critics who have the best wine magazines. They're mostly paying for our connections."[6]

Hearing Hubert de Boüard boast of his family's eight generations in Saint-Émilion shows how much this milieu is closed off and interrelated. Newcomers who can offer only their talent have their work cut out for them. A Frenchman born in Algeria, Thunevin was dismissed as a foreigner for years, even though he grew up alongside the château owners. Derenoncourt, a former laborer who is the son of blue-collar parents from the north, will never be completely accepted by the milieu.

The primary network is, of course, based on possible access to Robert Parker. This is one of the attractions of Rolland, the most important of the jet-set winemakers. They all try to lure the American into their web. This year, for the first time since his wine was classified *A*, Hubert de Boüard managed to do it. "He" came to Angélus in person. Hubertus Magnus is very proud of it. It's a double achievement: classification and becoming a required stop for Parker. For Hubert de Boüard, the stakes were high: now that his clients have obtained classification, what else could he offer them to keep them in his orbit other than Parker?

When you're a famous winemaker, a bad score from the master looks really bad. The owners expect results. And when they don't get them, you get a scolding, at least. Sometimes you even get fired.

If everyone is so interested in the American guru, it's because he sells wine. "We're businessmen, not poets," as Michel Rolland bluntly puts it. "They expect us to make good wine, but especially to know how to sell it."[7] And his brand makes wine sell, even if no one expects him to handle all the wines he consults for personally. Who cares? They're buying his name.

That's what these fancy consultants have offered the new owners. They're the headliners the financiers needed to make their vineyards exist. It wasn't hard to convince their clientele of this since they're mostly from the business world and they know only too well how essential reputation and brand creation are for launching a "product." "Today these people want to put their assets into a solid sector, so they hire a guru to make their wine so they can brag that they make the best wine in the world. And that's you how make your money grow,"[8] summarizes Dominique Techer, the last farmer on the Pomerol plateau. A Bordeaux press agent agrees: "They put together their team the way a director casts a movie; they need the prettiest actress, the most bankable leading man, and a good screenwriter. And once you've got the savoir faire, you just have to spread the word!"

Pierre Lurton, the aristocratic manager of the legendary Cheval Blanc and Yquem, has nothing but bad things to say about these consultants. Yet he uses one, the white wine specialist Denis Dubourdieu. What does he have against these winemakers? They're not around enough, they don't set foot on a daily basis on the soil of the vineyards they work for, and, finally, they're not credible. But, in fact, Cheval (the connoisseurs don't call it Cheval Blanc, just Cheval, emphasizing the last syllable) already has an ambassador, a main attraction who better than anyone knows how to sell his brand. And this man, who also happens to be delightful, is Pierre Lurton himself. He's the consultant for Bernard Arnault's châteaux. You only had to hear him relate in minute detail, to a table of handpicked journalists—among the guests was the head of communications for a major French television network—the receptions given by Cheval for

Bono, Vladimir Putin, or the king of Jordan, to understand that this château doesn't need any other consultant besides him. He gave Putin meaningful vintages, such as the year of his rise to power (the legendary 2000) and a bottle from the year each of his children was born. The Russian market is significant and Lurton's talent is that he can do business without seeming to, employing masterful strategy while being a magnificent host. He makes a polished impression and, in the exceedingly sophisticated French of the highborn, he adds, "It is true that the company [LVMH] does like to call on me when holding events for other brands, asking that I might set up a modest little refreshment area"[9]—where only the best vintages of Cheval or Yquem will be served.

Pleasing the opinion makers is thus an integral part of the job. You must be identified, known, recognized, and, if possible, raved about. During the last Bordeaux *en primeur* sales, all the special newspaper editions made it seem as if there were only three winemakers in all of France: Hubert de Boüard, Stéphane Derenoncourt, and Michel Rolland.

Basically, they court the journalists who help them out, and that's how this little wine world works. In media rankings, you always find the same names. Hubert de Boüard was named man of the year in 2013 by the *Revue du Vin de France* and was also (a few weeks later) named one of the two hundred wine personalities of the wine world, at number fifteen. Stéphane Derenoncourt came in at number twenty-six. Michel Rolland and Jean-Luc Thunevin were "only" numbers thirty-three and forty-six, respectively—relegated to the rank of "influential" while the first two were "essential."

Now the winemakers are brands themselves. We've come full circle.

Jean-Luc Thunevin totally embraces this role of go-between: "That's what I'm paid for; that's what you call consulting. I'm not the only one who does it. Michel Rolland has always done this after-sale work. He's not just an oenologist. He also presents the wines he consults for to the media. Rolland knows that giving advice about wine isn't enough. You also have to help people with promotion, which helps with sales. It's part of the package."[10]

Basically, journalists want to identify a man (or a woman) who can tell them a story. This new kind of guru does so with panache. Of course, sometimes those who tell good stories make mediocre wine. Too bad for the small winemakers who are not as eloquent.

"But to remain important, you always have to find something new. You discover a barrel that makes wine differently. You communicate about it to show that you're the kind who tracks down the latest innovations . . . Except that once you've communicated about it, everyone gets into it and you have to find something else if you want to stay on top. Otherwise you're dead,"[11] Jean-Luc Thunevin explains coolly.

Hubert de Boüard shares this deep-rooted anxiety: "It's really tough to always have new ideas. We're perpetually rushing ahead."[12]

However, the man isn't lacking for ideas. His latest discovery? Putting his wine upside down! At his château La Fleur de Boüard in Lalande-de-Pomerol, he installed sublime upside-down conical vats. Instead of being placed on the ground, the vats hang from the ceiling. Of course, since they're falling from the sky, the wine must be much better! It seems that the journalists from *La Vigne* magazine were blown away by this ingenious idea. The excited editors gave him two pages to promote this initiative.[13] But what does it do for the quality of the wine?

Not much, according to Pascal Chatonnet, oenologist and head of the Excell research laboratory in Bordeaux. "Every period has its fashion: stainless steel vats, wooden vats, egg-shaped vats, and now it's the vortex, because it's sexier to talk about a vortex . . . There were already conical vats but, look, now they're upside down! That changes everything!" he adds jokingly. "The thing is, you always need something new to create buzz and make the journalists happy."[14]

In this world, people spy on each other, are jealous of each other, and spend their time and energy trying to steal other people's clients. What a victory when you get hold of such and such a *grand cru*! Right now people are turning away from Rolland, who's beginning to seem like an aging star with young guns eager to carve up his empire. Though they're careful not to knock the general's statue down too quickly. In fact, the consultants' clients are really in control, elevating some, rejecting others, and changing horses to follow the fashion. Stéphane Derenoncourt does not really enjoy this game. Being an object that the owners can buy or toss out as they see fit doesn't appeal to him. He's well known for his explosive temper and his clients know there is a line they can't cross. Once a year (or more often, depending on his mood), this strong-willed northerner fires clients he finds too annoying or bothersome. However, not everyone has this luxury. Laurent Benoit, who used to raise black Gascon pigs and now works for Hubert de Boüard, recognizes that "some people don't look so closely at their clients' pedigrees; not everyone can afford to do so."[15] If the fighting is so rough, it's because the financial stakes are huge.

In France, these stars charge between €10,000 and €45,000 per year for their services. But all these alchemists establish their reputations in Bordeaux in order to be able to sell them better abroad. "Why do you think they take these international jobs? They go there two or three times a year. Michel Rolland has a thing in Argentina; he goes there once every two years. It's a jackpot! You can make a hundred and fifty thousand euros for an international contract. And since you can't keep up with the estates the way you do here, since the people can't call you and ask for your help continually, you have a lot less hassle for way more cash!" an expert who prefers to stay in Bordeaux summarizes with a smile. Derenoncourt gets €130,000 for contracts in India and up to €150,000 in China. When you consult for a hundred or so estates all over the world, it starts to turn into a nice little business.

Naturally, at these prices, competition is tough. And when you've turned your skill into a brand, why not keep on making money off your name? Recently, they've all started lines of low-end wines and put their valuable monikers on them.

Hubert de Boüard has stuck with religious metaphors. After Angélus for the *grand cru*, his lesser wines are called Revelations by Hubert de Boüard. As simple as that. Derenoncourt plays it more modestly by invoking the terroir with his wine Les Parcelles. But in both cases, they're selling their names on hundreds of thousands of bottles: the rights to the name, a percentage of sales, and the consulting charges. The wine merchants expect these big names to help them sell their hundreds of thousands of hectoliters of modest vintages.

These winemakers are a bit like the Karl Lagerfelds of wine, which the wine industry's version of Kering's François Pinault or LVMH's Bernard Arnault display as headliners. They certainly have talent, but they're bought for the commercial power of their names, to launch brands, and to increase prices. With Rolland's name on it, the wine is always worth more. They make different versions with this name and this brand: just as Lagerfeld was sold at H&M, Derenoncourt is sold at the supermarket chain Auchan for €4.50. Ordinary mortals thus feel their dreams are in reach, while they're actually buying a frozen entrée printed with the name of a three-star chef.

"Rolland never considered himself a magician but an added signature to help with the sale of the wines he consults for,"[16] Jean-Luc Thunevin serenely explains. The question that remains unanswered is the following: do all these winemakers who advise so many estates still sell wine with their names? Brands have mysterious—and lucrative—ways, it seems.

8

That Hide a
Dangerous Secret

February 14, 2013: a shy, slender man has shown up this morning to face a group of journalists who have come to hear a lecture by researcher Pascal Chatonnet, head of the Excell research laboratory, on pesticide residues in wine.

He's calm and assured. He doesn't look anything like a fiery activist. The vineyards he's in charge of aren't even organic. His name is Alain Dourthe and he manages the vines of Silvio Denz, the owner of Lalique, a man who called on architect Mario Botta to build a cathedral worthy of his wines. This unassuming man reigns over five châteaux and 120 hectares of grapes. He's not at all a rebellious hippie. He knows he is part of a grand tradition.

Therefore his cold fury is all the more surprising. His profession's code of silence concerning the issue of pesticide residues in wine is as incomprehensible to him as it is unacceptable. And this morning he's come to speak out. For many years he has tried to follow responsible farming practices. He's trying any way he can to reduce the number of pesticides used. And he takes a certain amount of pride in it. So much, in fact, that he decided that when he applied for the most recent Saint-Émilion classification, it would be a bonus to bring proof that his wines are not full of chemicals. So he had the last ten vintages of the two estates up for classification analyzed. He wanted to show the classification commission that "all the wines I've produced for ten years were free of pesticides."

Except that, to his great surprise, this wasn't the case. "In all the bottles before 2005, we found insecticides and especially antibotrytis chemicals [botrytis is a fungus that attacks the grapevines]. Starting then, we stopped using these products, and there are no more traces of them in our bottles." He is clearly shaken up. "It sends shivers up my spine. I was told that the yeasts used in wine making broke down the pesticides, absorbed them in some way, but the reality is here. The numbers speak for themselves,"[1] he says, all in one breath.

"Since 1999, we've been systematically checking for pesticides on our grapes before harvesting. No one's ever asked us for the results. No one cares. The profession wants nothing to do with the results we're giving them on the absence of pesticides in our wines,"[2] rails this winemaker who has been snubbed by his peers.

It's even more infuriating that these environmentally ethical practices, which cost more and are more labor-intensive, aren't valued at all by the Bordeaux wine trade, which instead prioritizes keeping costs down as much as possible.

Why do these wine analyses concern the industry so little? Because wine enjoys a level of impunity that is hard to believe. Indeed, it's one of the only products exempt from maximum residue limits. These are required of our fruits and vegetables, our flours and our breads, but not our wine.

The wine industry is required to abide by maximum residue limits only for grapes. Basically, they're happy to look at how many pesticides are on the grapes before they're made into wine (though in practice, this analysis isn't performed), but once it's in the bottle, monitoring ends. As if all the residues evaporated through the magic of Bacchus!

Plus, the famous MRLs (maximum residue limits) for grapes are excessively high and absolutely inadequate. To put it simply, if you ever find MRLs in wine that are higher than what's allowed on the grapes, it means that the winemaker used them with an extremely heavy hand.

"It's almost hypocritical," admits Pascal Chatonnet. "Everyone knows perfectly well that the limits are way too high."[3] In fact, this researcher suggested to his clients that they could voluntarily set their own MRLs for wine. He established limits for residues in wine that are ten to a thousand times lower than the limits for residues on grapes. "Why? Because wine making is an extremely efficient process for eliminating residue, so there's simply no reason to find levels in the wine that are close or equal to or even just slightly lower than those of the grapes."[4] He allows a mixture of a maximum of five fungicides, whose total can't be above .05mg/kg, which is still one hundred times more than what is allowed in tap water. However, despite the rather flexible nature of this self-regulation, most of the wines he analyzed during his last study wouldn't have been able to get his quality label. So there's a problem. This scandal has been carefully hushed up until now.

Pascal Chatonnet doesn't understand why the industry is so reticent in this regard. He's convinced that the way things are headed we'll end up with restrictive legislation. Meanwhile, he observes that the MRLs are set by politicians who don't want to rub anyone the wrong way—especially not economic titans as powerful as those in the wine industry— instead of by objective scientists.

This researcher may not like it, but, for now, the industry's strategy is to keep silent. And Pascal Chatonnet's frankness "riles people up," as he admits himself. "The Interprofessional Council of Bordeaux Wines is staunchly opposed to what we're doing. They're beside themselves that we're taking on a topic that they've decided to hush up."[5]

But nothing will stop this determined scientist. "When you do this job, either you decide to work or you decide to do politics. We decided to work,"[6] he says proudly. In fact, his lab participated in a large-scale project launched by the French Wine-Making Institute to examine wines from all over France with a fine-tooth comb. The institute never made the results public. "They think that everything gets repeated in alarmist fashion," says Pascal Chatonnet regretfully. "When the French Wine-Making Institute ordered this analysis, it was scolded by the Interprofessional Council.

Since the Interprofessional Council funds them . . . They preferred to drop it,"[7] the researcher says.[8]

Pesticides—what pesticides? Sometimes the industry's policy of covering up is almost ridiculous. At Pascal Chatonnet's lecture, a scientist from the French Wine-Making Institute came to present the results of his research showing that better meteorological information can reduce the use of pesticides. It was quite a positive study showing that the industry is trying to do better. Nothing subversive, in any case. Despite the innocence of the topic, the researcher's supervisors didn't allow him to publish his presentation or to circulate the video that was made of it.

Yet nothing arouses more suspicion than a cover-up. It seemed that the enchanted kingdom's law of silence had been broken by the 2005 publication of the extensive study (from 1990 to 2003) by the Agriculture Ministry's directorate general for food : 1,122 wine samples were analyzed for pesticide residues. The study revealed that out of ten active substances applied by winegrowers to the soil, five had a chance of being found on the grapes and three in the wine. This study was launched for political reasons: French wines had been stopped at the American border because they contained a substance called procymidone, a fungicide. So, once again, it wasn't an issue of public health but endangered markets. And since then? Silence.

Although no international legislation exists, some countries are still more particular than France. For example, Switzerland established a very restrictive MRL for a fungicide that's widely used in winegrowing.[9] Japan also has stricter standards.

"I don't understand my colleagues!" Alain Dourthe cries. "The majority of *grands crus classés* sell eighty-five percent of their wine abroad. How can they continue to live with this sword of Damocles hanging over their heads?"[10] Perhaps because they know perfectly well that they have every chance of slipping by. "There's not enough monitoring at customs. And when goods are blocked, it's usually for political reasons. The countries we export to only check the shipments when they want to put pressure on," says Pascal Chatonnet. "That's what China did in 2013. They claimed that since certain endocrine disruptors[11] and phthalates were now banned in France, no traces of them should be found in the alcohol we sold them. But this is all theater. It's tit for tat: if you hassle me about what I export to you, then I'll do the same thing with your products,"[12] the researcher says. So China blocked containers of cognac at the border. And panic hit all the French *grands crus*, who quickly stormed the research laboratories.

Then the crisis passed and the industry went back to its regular position. "It's an ostrich policy, that's for sure. You stick your head in the sand and don't see the problem, so you claim there isn't one,"[13] Chatonnet says wryly.

Of course, this strategy annoys many people. Some who challenge the system and advocate for transparency regularly publish wine analyses in the press. The first organization to attack this disturbing wine industry exception was an antipesticide NGO, Générations Futures. These activists want to uncover the impact of these products on our health and the environment.

On March 26, 2008, they published a groundbreaking study of forty bottles of wine from France, Austria, Germany, Italy, Portugal, South Africa, Australia, and Chile. The result? One hundred percent of conventionally grown wines were contaminated. The study had especially targeted prestigious Burgundy wines, as well as Pomerol. The names of the estates were not revealed for fear of lawsuits. Plus, the idea wasn't to get particular vineyards in trouble, but to show that under the current state of legislation some wines didn't deserve their reputations. The study showed residues from over four different chemical products per bottle, with the most affected wines containing up to fourteen. In some of the wines tested, the NGO found doses that were fifty-eight hundred times greater than those allowed in drinking water. Should we be surprised when we know that the French wine industry is responsible for almost 20 percent of the nation's pesticide and fungicide use while covering only about 3 percent of the country's farmland? And that France, as the *New York Times*[14] pointed out in shock, is the number one user of pesticides in Europe?

In December 2009[15] and then in March 2010, it was the *Revue du Vin de France*'s turn to analyze four 2004 bottles from four different regions: Château Canon, a Saint-Émilion *premier grand cru classé*; Goldert, a *grand cru* from the Zind-Humbrecht estate; Les Caillerets, a Volnay *premier cru* by Bouchard Père et Fils; and a Château de Pibarnon red Bandol. In the Saint-Émilion, they found two chemical fungicides[16] as well as copper. In March of the same year, they wondered if "pesticides were soluble over time."[17] Their conclusion? A certain number of chemicals would have dissolved, except for iprodione.[18] Wines from the 1990s contain not only this fungicide but also insecticides.

"That's logical," says Pascal Chatonnet. "Procymidone[19] and iprodione are substances that were widely used and are almost indestructible. You find them in champagne thirty years later!"[20]

Chatonnet monitors pesticides in his lab and regularly studies a wide range of about three hundred samples. In his latest study on wines from southern France (including Bordeaux), 90 percent of those he analyzed had pesticide residue. Some had as many as nine pesticides in them, usually fungicides.

Chatonnet points out that the results show improvement from his previous study. "Six years ago, we found up to twelve chemicals per bottle with an average of nine; in the last results, the average was five or six. It's still a lot but it represents significant progress. The question is this: why do we find five chemicals when in practice you can manage wine production with two or three?"[21] It was after drawing these conclusions that the scientist suggested his clients limit themselves to a smaller number of products to treat their vines.

In particular, he doesn't want to see traces of any herbicides, insecticides, or acaricides, which he considers dangerous for the local plant life.

Chatonnet also wonders about the presence of banned chemicals in the wines he analyzed. "In 2009, we found 0.3

milligrams of carbendazim in wine. How can we explain such a concentration of pesticides when this substance is banned?[22] Not to mention that when it's used on grapes, it's definitely found in wine: its grape–wine transfer rate is one hundred percent."[23]

These results are confirmed by the most recent analysis by the consumer association UFC Que Choisir. This organization examined ninety-two bottles from Bordeaux, Burgundy, Champagne, Côtes du Rhône, Languedoc-Roussillon, etc. It detected carbendazim in nineteen samples! One hundred percent of the wines were contaminated, both conventional wines and organic wines (only trace amounts, but they were still contaminated by their polluted neighbors). The association singled out two Bordeaux: Mouton Cadet 2010,[24] which beat all the records with fourteen pesticides, and a white Graves, Château Roquetaillade Le Bernet 2011,[25] which contained about five times more residues than other Bordeaux tested and is already much more loaded with residues than other French wines.[26]

While all regions were criticized, Bordeaux appears the most polluted, followed by Champagne, and then, to a lesser degree, Burgundy.

These results correspond to the 2013 data from Agreste, the statistical service of the Agriculture Ministry. The wine-making region that uses chemicals the most is Bordeaux with a treatment frequency index of 38.5. Next is Pyrénées-Orientales (32), Provence-Alpes-Côte d'Azur (29.4), Champagne (28.4), and Beaujolais (28.1). Quite far behind is Burgundy (24.7).

These fine wines will continue to have residues if they keep avoiding self-regulation in the use of pesticides. And how do these chemically treated wines taste?

As usual, this brings us to one of the vicious cycles that are typical of conventional agriculture. One of the best oenologists in Champagne, Hervé Jestin, who specializes in organic wine making, explains the slightly absurd strategy that wines filled with chemical products must rely on. "Once you have residues, fermentation quality is lower and the wines are less pure. Most of the chemicals used are fungicides. Yeast, which is a fungus, doesn't like this kind of product."[27] So what to do? Add industrial yeasts!

This is the magic of modern oenology, which can provide winemakers with turnkey solutions to replace what the pesticides have eradicated.

You won't see any sign of these additives or residues on the labels of our fine wines. This divine nectar is not subject to the laws that apply to the common folk.

9

Maintained by
Curious Methods

She's small and charming and welcomes you with a big smile. She shows you around her lab proudly. She's Magali Grinbaum, the head of pesticide analysis at the French Wine-Making Institute. In other words, a watchdog planted inside the system. She's known as Madame Residues. She spreads industry gospel about this thorny problem. She's at the front lines when articles come out on the topic and she also helps the vineyard owners make all traces of these products disappear from their wines. Today she's supposed to give a lecture to a group of independent winemakers. The title of her lecture is "Residues of Chemical Products in Wine? Oenological Methods of Reducing Them." Ms. Grinbaum is a kind of magician who makes problems disappear like rabbits from her hat.

Despite her interesting topic, no one showed up. Yet her talk was edifying. She listed the pesticides with the highest risk of turning up in wine. Then she described many experiments to make them appear to vanish using oenological products. Her conclusion? Charcoal works pretty well, but the color of the wine vanishes too. In other words, the methods aren't yet totally foolproof.

It's quite amusing to see all the energy expended by the industry as well as the national, regional, and departmental authorities—even if they deny it—to fund research that's in part about perfecting camouflage techniques.

Instead of reforming farming methods, let's just hide the residues as much as we can. That's the strategy of winemakers and the government.

This game of hide-and-seek begins well before the wine-making process. The winemakers understand that in these environmentally correct times, it looks bad to openly acknowledge the use of chemical products. Of course, some still do. It's astonishing to see, for example, how the spring soil in the prestigious Pomerol appellation is red with herbicides. Since the winemaker feels that he should shift to something more environmental, he uses little capsules of sexual hormones to trap certain grape predators and thus avoids using insecticides. The soil is napalmed from below but the branches are draped with these eco-friendly tools to give the locals the impression that he's green.

This practice greatly annoys Dominique Techer, an organic winemaker on this famous appellation. "How in Pomerol, the land of fine wines sold for thirty to three hundred euros, can people still be doing this kind of thing? They just have to stop buying new SUVs so often and farm their land a bit better! It's unacceptable that the taxpayers have to pay to clean up the water for people who are living in high style!"[1]

Those who openly acknowledge being polluters are few and far between. In renowned vineyards, it's now considered good form to camouflage soil treated with weed killers. The latest fashion is to plow the soil that's been treated to hide the harmful effects of herbicides. "It gets better," says Dominique Techer. "There are those who only work the soil properly right around the château and for the rest of their land it's chemical warfare. They take out the heavy artillery,"[2] says the winemaker scornfully. "Then they can take some nice photos and make a great brochure boasting about how much they care about the environment."[3]

Such methods aren't limited to Pomerol. In the top Saint-Émilion *premiers crus*, it's the same story. The winemaker Stéphane Derenoncourt laughed at my surprise, saying sardonically: "In any case, herbicides aren't banned. You should know now that for the classification, it's better to have a nice parking lot than to stop using weed killer!"[4]

PR works wonders. But making real efforts to change, that's another story. Dominique Techer remembers with amusement a big open house organized by a prestigious château in the area. The estate wanted to show off its beehives, which are excellent signs that the owners care about the environment. The journalists who came that day heard a very touching story: these bees were protected because they could gather pollen from all the wild grasses left by these bighearted winemakers. Except that "the soil around the grapevines was treated with weed killer! The beehives were in the wooded part of the château!"⁵ laughs Dominique Techer.

Some Bordeaux residents have a gift for staging worthy of the greatest filmmakers. But does this talent exempt them from being honest with consumers?

10

Praised by an
Enthusiastic Court

In the midst of the vino business kingdom, with its adulterated INAO, its vineyard owners eager to make their investments pay off, and its consultants of all kinds, there is also another powerful force: the critics.

Jean-Luc Thunevin puts it quite simply: "We need them and they need us."[1] Critics bring fame and get the wines' names out there so their readers hear about them and want to buy one instead of the other. They are thus essential to this game of poker. But their power is less important than they think.

In this inner circle, Parker's in his own league, leaving other critics far behind. "I don't even know why they come to taste, because the only one who really counts is Parker. These outsiders whine and complain about how hard it is to test so many wines . . . Why don't they just stop! We don't care about their opinion!"[2] This blunt advice is from Pascal Chatonnet, winemaker and oenologist, but all Bordeaux shares it. This Gaulish village knows that there is only one druid who has the recipe for the magic potion that makes wines sell for a fortune.

The other critics are well aware of this hierarchy, and thus they follow in the master's steps. Parker tastes very early, generally in mid-March for wines harvested the previous October, which, in fact, annoys the winemakers. "If he could taste in August, even before the harvest, he would do it!" grumbles a dissatisfied winemaker. Therefore, the other critics come right after Parker, respecting the priority the guru deserves. This year, only one critic decided to compete with Parker by choosing the exact same dates: Jean-Marc Quarin, a local critic who edits the wine site Quarin.com. Why taste at the same time as God? "To see if I'll be received the same way he is."[3]

And especially in the same conditions. For there are dreadfully fierce rivalries and cutthroat competition among wine critics. Pascal Chatonnet of the Excell laboratory remembers a famous scene at Cos d'Estournel, a *grand cru* belonging to Michel Reybier, the former sausage king. After the château recently added a large tasting room, the big-name critics were very displeased that less important critics could taste at the same time they did. They demanded that the owner make these "losers" leave the room when they were present.[4]

The winemakers are careful not to offend certain sensitive critics, even if they secretly laugh about this. "You have to watch out, because these people can have micropower over niche markets," says Jean-Luc Thunevin. "Jean-Marc

Quarin, for example, has influence over the Swiss market. You wouldn't know it but Switzerland is an important market, with wealthy people."[5] So don't make fun of them, even when their behavior is surprising. Pierre Lurton, the manager of Cheval Blanc, remembers mischievously the same critic, Jean-Marc Quarin, begging him one year to be present at the assemblage (blending) of his legendary *premier cru*. "He wanted to try and he concocted a little mixture in two seconds and said, 'I think it's really good.' Honestly, it was average. He came back during the *en primeur* sales and asked us if we were using his blend. I said no, we had made many others since then. He got annoyed and said, 'That's too bad. I would've given it a better score.'"[6] But surely he jests.

However, the media aren't pulling the strings; it's the owners and the three or four powerful winemakers. Any critics who get out of line will find themselves punished. If you write one or two bad reviews, or don't behave respectfully enough, you'll be exiled. And if the journalists are banned from the châteaux and no longer have the right to taste, what will they do? How can they do their job? "Because they can't buy the bottles we give them with their minimum wage salaries," sneers an important Bordeaux vineyard owner. Indeed, how could they do three or four tastings of a bottle of wine that sells for €300 to €1,000? How can they have access to the samples of the *en primeur* sales when they aren't yet for sale?

"The critics realize there's a red line they can't cross if they want to still be welcome at the châteaux. None of them will cross it,"[7] says Franck Dubourdieu, a former

Bordeaux wine merchant who is very knowledgeable about the industry. Basically, we shouldn't expect the critics to revolutionize the establishment or take foolish risks to point out the decreasing quality of a *grand cru classé*. "Thanks to us, these poor bums live like billionaires. Why should they bite the hand that feeds them?" this great winemaker tells me scornfully.

Jean-Luc Thunevin makes no apologies for the banishment he inflicted on "two or three journalists whom I refused to allow to taste Valandraud."[8] "I don't even want to name them; it would give them too much attention. At first, they tried to come back every year, but, after finding my door closed, they gave up. I told them it wasn't worth their trouble to come. 'Why do you want to taste? You don't enjoy it; you don't like what I do or what I am. So spare yourself this unpleasantness!'"[9]

Not being able to taste Valandraud when you call yourself a great critic is upsetting. It would be even worse if it were Pétrus, Ausone, or Cheval Blanc. So you put blinders on and support the icons. Too bad for the outsiders, who have little chance of emerging under this system. The way tastings take place also says a lot about the hidden hierarchies. You go to Cheval Blanc and Ausone, to Derenoncourt and Boüard. But you have the wine from everyone else—the small vineyards, the nobodies—delivered to your room so you can taste it, or not.

Breaking the glass ceiling when you're an unknown wine producer is extremely complicated. One winemaker described how distraught he was when James Molesworth,

James Suckling's successor at *Wine Spectator*, didn't taste his wine. Molesworth had even sent an astonishing e-mail to the wine producer: "Given the generally poor quality of the 2012 vintage," he wrote, "it wasn't necessary to go to his estate to taste his wine." James Molesworth didn't go to Angélus or Pavie either this year, even though they were both recently promoted to the highest rank of *premier grand cru classé A*. And since Hubert de Boüard and Gérard Perse, owner of Château Pavie, among others, refused to bring him their bottles, *Wine Spectator*'s readers didn't get scores for Angélus or Pavie. That's how far these battles will go.

Of course, wine critics may irritate you a bit when you're at the top of the hierarchy, but they can't stop you from existing. However, if you're at the bottom, surviving by creating a media presence is a huge challenge. That's the whole reason for having a big-name winemaker as your consultant. They are the go-betweens between you and the big critics. Everything happens behind the scenes, at dinners or lunches where truffles are served with fine wines. The guru introduces the great journalist(s) to his clients, who receive them with all the respect due to their rank. Everyone does this kind of lobbying. The only one who talks about it openly, as usual, is Jean-Luc Thunevin. "That's part of my job. I have dinners. I introduce my clients to the critics who count in a relaxed, casual atmosphere."[10] He sends a clear message to the journalists: the people he's introducing them to rely on him. The journalists should treat them as they would the winemaker himself: with interest and, if possible, indulgence. The network must function whatever the cost. And in this region, with its history of Freemasonry, we know how important unofficial connections are.

As for the journalists, they are sometimes receptive to these indulgences. Sometimes in their excitement they slip up. For instance, a reporter from a French magazine was so pleased to have been invited to fly business class to Lebanon to visit a vineyard that he took a photo of his plane ticket and posted it to his Facebook page. Nice treatment that was rewarded with a full page of coverage!

So are all the critics bought off? "There are some who are for sale, anyway!" smiles Jean-Luc Thunevin. "There's a journalist who's well known in the industry who writes a good review if you give him five thousand euros. I like having them in my pocket."[11]

Except for a few black sheep, the profession might be exemplary. Of course, its attention is still focused on those who know how to invest wisely.

"The critics don't come here because we don't buy advertising. It's all about quid pro quo," grumbles Dominique Techer, the last farmer on the Pomerol plateau. "Basically, if you want articles, you have to scratch their backs. So either you have a big PR budget and they talk about you, or you're not part of all that rigmarole and they don't come to you. Or only rarely, since they still want to look objective and represent all the styles. So from time to time they'll condescend to write about a lesser-known wine to make the readers think they taste everything. But don't be fooled."[12]

"The bigger you are, the more they expect you to spend on advertising," Jean-Luc Thunevin admits. "When I consulted for Château La Dominique, I told them they had to invest at least three hundred thousand euros a year in communications."[13]

That's the price you have to pay to be talked about and to exist in the classifications and top-twenty lists of the wine media.

There are also lots of little businesses that these critics or magazines can get involved in thanks to all their connections.

The *Revue du Vin de France* invites winegrowers to participate in its wine shows. This kind of event where the winemakers bring their wine for free, pay for their booths, and cover their travel expenses, and the attendees pay to get in, certainly improves their bottom line. "Refusing to go and pay for a booth means taking a chance that they won't like you as much next time," confides a winemaker who prefers to cover himself by getting a big booth.

But the *Revue du Vin de France* isn't the only one involved in this kind of thing. Far from it. The prestigious *Wine Spectator* also puts on the New York Wine Experience, a little tasting program that costs $1,875 per person for connoisseurs, which gives you an idea of how much they must charge the winemakers attending. For winemakers the conditions are the same in Paris or New York: you pay for it all—with a smile!

Every year, the critics Bettane and Desseauve, who work in tandem, offer their Grand Tasting at the Carrousel du Louvre. Saying no to them is unthinkable when you know how many magazines these great men write for.

As for James Suckling, he's become a real business-man. He regularly organizes huge events in Hong Kong. An entrance ticket costs $6,000 for winemakers and $750 for "select wine drinkers" who participate. This is a sector that's doing fantastically in the midst of a worldwide recession.

11

A Very Nice Carnival

In mid-April, the excitement in Bordeaux is at its peak. It's the time when everyone is here. Welcome to wine's fashion week, where hot-button issues such as classifications, pesticides, and other gray areas are all off the table. As in the fashion world, it's clear that the master already knows what's what. Plus, he already came to taste one month earlier. The merchants and all the big importers have already had their premiere. In other words, most of the deals are done, until the crowning glory, Parker's scores, which come out, as always, at the end of the month.

But even if the *en primeur* sales are a gigantic farce, it's unthinkable for any self-respecting merchant or wine journalist not to be there. It's the place to be to maintain your network, to go to fancy dinners and lavish parties, and show the world that you're part of the crème de la crème.

So the wine world rushes to Bordeaux to taste the samples that have been tailor-made for the visitors. The samples are the wines from October's harvest that are tasted in April. These wines are much too young to really be appreciated, but a handful of critics or experts are supposed to be able to spot their future potential. "It's guesswork. They show me babies, and I have to guess if they'll become Olympic champion javelin throwers, pianists, teachers, or politicians," James Suckling describes it, waxing poetic. In any case, the baby must be good-looking and in the best shape possible to attract future buyers.

The consultants run frantically from one vineyard and one estate to the next, making sure everything is perfect and offering carefully prepared samples to the press, the importers, and the merchants.

Stéphane Derenoncourt compares these wines to pretty dolls specially prepared for the event. The dolls have been prematurely aged and made appealing for this crucial week. "They're babies that have to be trained, educated, and civilized,"[1] summarizes Jean-Philippe Fort, a consulting oenologist at Rolland's lab who believes one must accept the fashion week atmosphere. "At a fashion show, you make sure the girls are beautiful and in good shape so the dresses will look divine on them. With wine, it's the same thing."[2]

Everyone has tricks up their sleeves to make those prepubescent girls the most beautiful in the world. And since Bordeaux wines are assemblages (blends) of different batches (different plots of land, different barrels), the first "trick" is to offer only the batches that taste the best—even if you know perfectly well that for the final assemblage of the wine, i.e., what the consumer will buy, all the batches, even those that were rejected for the *en primeur* sales because they didn't taste quite good enough, will go in the bottle. Basically, for tasting you offer only the very best, but you'll sell a blend of everything.

Jean-Philippe Fort defends the practice, saying, "It's not deceptive." He explains that if he removes one or two batches that will be present in the final assemblage, it's only because they don't taste right at that specific moment, that they're not smooth or sexy enough. "The people who come to taste, the journalists and the professionals, won't be able to understand these subtleties."[3]

Basically, you have to impress the journalists—them again—who aren't competent or imaginative enough for you to show them the reality of the wine at a specific time. So you have to blow them away with a wine that's especially made for them, which, ultimately, isn't the one you'll sell to consumers. Another strange practice of the enchanted kingdom.

Some estates even offer samples that have been put together especially for a particular journalist. In an article in *Decanter*,[4] Yann Bouscasse, the owner of Château Cantinot, reveals that he makes samples from new barrels for American journalists, who are supposed to like their wine more full-bodied and oaky. Then he makes samples using old barrels for the Europeans.

"It's well known and it's always been done," smiles a defrocked winemaker who had to sell his vineyards after an estate battle. "Most of the winemakers make tailor-made samples to please one journalist or another!"

"It's a deal for willing fools," Dominique Techer, the rebellious farmer of the Pomerol plateau, says ironically. "It's a mass lie. When you want to marry off an ugly daughter, you need to fix her up a bit. So you make her pretty. Once you get her home, you discover the fake boobs. The deal is intrinsically like that from the beginning. The fool is the final customer, the people who read the scores and think that it means something."[5]

Jean-Luc Thunevin sees it differently. For him, the scam of making fabulous samples for the *en primeur* market when the bottled wines are mediocre is short-lived. "Some wines do it, it seems. Of course, we know they do. But it's a little game you can play once or twice, but not three times. Your credibility is at stake. A very good *en primeur* wine where the final customer systematically says it's mediocre, that can't last."[6] Plus, self-respecting *grands crus* often have better scores when bottled than what they got *en primeur*. The problem is that the big deals are made in April. And the winemaker's year is at stake with those scores. If the wine is rewarded later, that's nice, but it's often too late.

In any case, you have to keep the journalists in your pocket. Plus, to be sure that they don't lose their way, you can direct them to the events organized by the biggest estates. Basically, you make samples for the journalists that they can appreciate and you take them to targeted places that they can identify.

The Right Bank Circle, the Union of Grands Crus, and, of course, the *en primeur* sales of Rolland, Derenoncourt, and now the all-important Boüard. Each consultant flexes his muscles to show off his protégés. Two hundred fifty for Rolland, almost one hundred for Derenoncourt, and about fifty for Boüard. Sometimes the protégés aren't even around. Rolland makes no bones about it: it's the Rolland brand that counts, not the wine producers. Many of these winemakers have disappeared entirely behind the brand of their consultant.

"It's a somewhat incomprehensible game of supply, demand, connections, scores, and cronyism, and it's called the Bordeaux *en primeur* market," laughs Jean-Luc Thunevin. "It's worked well for a long time and it's the envy of the whole world. It's huge in terms of image, money, and reputation."[7] Since this is wine's fashion week, attended by elite stars, everyone knows how important presentation is. Jean-Luc Thunevin makes €3 million in revenue every year at this time. So you could say that at those prices, it's in his interest not to mess up his samples.

Why try so hard to make this presentation a success and impress the participants if it isn't to sell your wine at the highest price possible? For behind these questions of taste, this is mostly pure business at work. The *en primeur* market is huge. It concerns only 5 percent or 6 percent of Bordeaux wines, but it represents the highest financial volumes. And who is its best or in fact its only trader? Parker, yet again. His scores set the prices. Recently, Liv-ex, the wine stock market, has really taken off. Originally, the *en primeur* market was simply a somewhat virtual market in which the winemakers could make money by selling wines that would be delivered to the clients after aging for two years. Now it's become a whole speculative system. In the past, the client who took the risk of buying early and had the patience to wait was rewarded by paying a bit less. But the idea, ultimately, was still to drink the wine, not to try to get rich by betting on an insane rise in prices.

Today, people play the market with fine wines as with risky stocks. Plus, some vineyard owners think they aren't making enough money on the deal and have gotten out of the *en primeur* market to reap the incredible profits all alone instead of sharing them with merchants and others. In particular, that's the case with the legendary Château Latour, a *premier grand cru classé* in 1855 that is owned by François Pinault. It must be said that the money is insane since some vintages have smashed the ceiling. But the bubble is starting to burst now that the prices no longer make sense. Bordeaux's eyes were bigger than its stomach when it realized there was a way to take advantage of China's thing for red wine. In fact, the auctions have gradually moved to Asia. Parker caught on when he sold his magazine to investors from Singapore. As for Suckling, he spends half the year doing business in Hong Kong.

Thus the Chinese control the *en primeur* market, although they don't get directly involved in it, preferring to go through intermediaries in London, Zurich, or Hong Kong. Prices have skyrocketed. Thanks to buyers' delusions of grandeur, some fine wines are snapped up for €7,000 or €8,000. But the tide is turning. And bottles of Lafite Rothschild that had reached up to ten times their original price for the '82 vintage—Parker's "birth" vintage—are now losing

30 percent of their value. "The Chinese realize they have bought at much higher prices than everyone else. They have the unpleasant feeling of having been had,"[8] says Gérard Margeon, Alain Ducasse's sommelier.

It's the last straw. Now, the wine stored in these distant lands hangs over Bordeaux *grands crus* like the sword of Damocles. "I visited the old military tunnels in Hong Kong," Gérard Margeon relates. "They're filled to the top with wine. The idea is certainly to bring it out some day. There's a lot of wine there, and the market is growing less quickly than anticipated."[9]

Indeed, this is enough to make Bordeaux winemakers worry. It's highly unlikely that the Chinese investors will continue to buy on a massive scale if the results aren't up to snuff.

12

Bordeaux Is Booming in China

For one week every two years, Vinexpo, the international wine show, opens its doors. It's another important event on the circuit. During Vinexpo, it's impossible to find a hotel room in Bordeaux for less than €300. There are no more prix fixe meals in the restaurants; it's à la carte or nothing. And the prices on the menu go up 30 percent. The people of Bordeaux await, grasping their cash registers, the thousands of Chinese visitors on whom they now depend. France exports almost 40 million gallons of wine to China every year, and Bordeaux gets the lion's share of this with 65 percent of these exports by value. In a few years, the country has become a veritable gold mine, leading the ecstatic Bordeaux wine producers to drop their traditional clients. Good-bye to the French, who are too poor. So long, you Americans, still recovering from the financial crisis. Hello, China!

Many do not share this enthusiasm. Stephan von Neipperg, a distinguished aristocrat who is the charismatic owner of *grands crus classés* in Saint-Émilion, can't get over it. Running into the arms of these newcomers is a mistake. With his piercing eyes and his Errol Flynn mustache, he rails against the short-term focus that has made many of his competitors fall for these buyers, at the risk of artificially inflating prices. "The Chinese are like the big-box stores. They take you, they become your only customer, and then they destroy you and throw you away."[1]

And now that the pipeline is full and the vats are filled to overflowing with red wine, these savvy traders seem to have become much more picky about their purchases. In some cases, they're selling off what they've just bought.

This market is complicated. All the owners of French *grands crus classés* are involved to some degree in lawsuits with unscrupulous businessmen in China who have registered the names of French brands over there. Their goal, of course, is to extort money from the owners. Basically, if you want to get your brand back, you have to go through my intermediary. Ausone and many others had to fight hard and get into interminable legal battles to get their names back. Alain Vauthier, the owner of Ausone, had to spend €100,000 to protect his brand.

"It's a real jungle," acknowledges Stéphane Derenoncourt. "It seems like their only goal is to make money as fast as possible at any cost."[2]

So it's not easy to keep control over your brand. And it's really hard to fight against counterfeits. Stephan von Neipperg proudly shows off the Bubble Tag system he purchased from a company called Prooftag. It features a tamper-resistant security seal with a randomly generated pattern of bubbles that can be verified online. The stakes are high. At a show in Beijing, a poster above the booths read: NO COUNTERFEIT WINES HERE!

Gérard Margeon, Alain Ducasse's sommelier, likes to show the photos he took last year at the Shanghai wine show. They show huge posters for the event with gigantic reproductions of the labels of the most prestigious French wines. But they're all fake! There are even misnomers such as Chatréal Latour and Lafite Cellar. It's the kingdom of the fakes.

"An empty bottle of Lafite Rothschild sells for eighty to a hundred euros in China," explains Neipperg. "People aren't spending that much on empty bottles just for the value of the glass!"[3] Now the winemakers break their bottles after every tasting. Lafite, which was the Holy Grail of the Chinese clientele for years, has seen its image tarnished by being counterfeited so many times. "No one in China dares to buy it anymore," one winemaker says. "People are too afraid of looking like hicks who bought fakes." In China, precious wines aren't primarily for drinking yourself but for giving as gifts to honor your host. So no one wants to risk a faux pas.

In addition to Bordeaux, Burgundy is also affected, as shown by the recent US trial of Zhen Wang Huang, better known as Rudy Kurniawan. This very wealthy businessman claimed to be Chinese or Indonesian, depending on whom he was talking to. For years, he fooled the greatest connoisseurs worldwide. He's said to have sold tens of millions of euros worth of fakes! His method was simple and almost flawless: he held lavish tastings of real wines to which he invited elite buyers, and then he sold them fakes. At his home in Los Angeles, the FBI discovered a whole workshop for fake labels and wines. A winemaker from Burgundy, Laurent Ponsot, caught on to the fraud. He was surprised to see bottles of his Clos Saint-Denis wine from the 1940s and 1950s up for auction in New York, since he started producing it only in 1982. He started investigating and traced the bottles back to Kurniawan. His detective work led to the arrest of one of the greatest counterfeiters of the century.

The Chinese market is not only tough, but also very much in flux: the big buyers of yesterday can disappear overnight. "Often, you get to the importer's office, and there's no wine sales team. The guys are selling wine but also apartments," says a troubled Bordeaux merchant. "One day, overnight, they'll get out of wine."

Patrick Bouey, a dapper fifty-something Bordeaux merchant who goes for long bike rides to clear his head, recently learned this the hard way. He describes the country as like quicksand, a place where fortunes are made and lost according to political favor or disgrace. He seems a bit lost in this foreign world that he nonetheless can't ignore. He admits that it's impossible today to get by without it: China has become the biggest market for Bordeaux. Over a few years, Patrick Bouey's business has followed the same path, putting its fate into the hands of a distant market. In three years, the business he does with China has gone from €300,000 to over €7.7 million today. Yet the country is a jungle. Last year, some of Bouey's most important clients ended up in prison. "It happens, but it's not the rule," explains Wei Xu, a talented young businessman from Shanghai who masterfully handles marketing for YesMyWine, one of the main Chinese online wine start-ups. Wearing an unforgettable pink suit and a salesman's smile, the keenly intelligent Wei admits that two-thirds of the people selling wine in China in recent years have disappeared. "All the better for us, the market is becoming professionalized! However, it's too bad for the French merchants, especially in Bordeaux, who bet on these people who are now insolvent."[4]

The Chinese adventure is risky. But you have to do it. It's a complicated undertaking to get into this fabulous market and thrive there. That's why Patrick Bouey dragged Stéphane Derenoncourt to China. Together, the two men launched a line of low-priced terroir wines called Les Parcelles. It's hard to ignore this huge potential market where you can sell hundreds of thousands of bottles. Bouey took Stéphane Derenoncourt around to all the start-ups. He's hoping that YesMyWine will be more reliable than his previous clients but, in the end, there's no way to be sure. Derenoncourt was led around from city to city, from one tasting to another, from lunch to dinner. He had his photo taken and signed bottles of wine like a rock star. This isn't just celebrity worship; signed bottles sell for a lot of money.

Jean-Luc Thunevin also does business in China. "They take pictures of you. They film you. They look at you with admiration, but you're there to work like a regular sales rep,"[5] he says bluntly.

Reluctantly, Stéphane Derenoncourt plays the celebrity wine-maker game. It must be torturous for this stern, quiet man, but he goes along with it. They all go along with it. They don't really have a choice. Wei is categorical: there always needs to be a little something extra to sell your wares in China. That little something is the winemaker himself.

"We had a contest for our best clients. Thirty thousand VIPs tried to click on the website as fast as possible to win a tasting with Stéphane Derenoncourt! About twenty people were selected that way—ten in Shanghai, ten in Beijing. And the Frenchman ran from city to city to offer himself to the Chinese market . . . It was perfect!" Wei says, delighted. "In China, we love competition, and the idea of winning a tasting with Derenoncourt is a big challenge. It created incredible buzz! Those who weren't there were jealous, and they fought harder to be selected the next time. This will inspire them to buy more and to be even more responsive to the events we launch. And since the people we invited are all nouveaux riches who are pretty satisfied with themselves, as soon as the tasting was over, they immediately posted about this wonderful time with the marvelous Stéphane in great detail on Weibo [the Chinese Twitter]. That's all free advertising for us!"[6] Wei Xu says with an eager grin.

This extremely complex market could thus turn away from Bordeaux as quickly as it has embraced it.

"It's sad for Bordeaux, but it's true that they're a bit out of fashion," Wei sighs a few weeks later in Beaune. "Now we want Burgundy, especially Romanée-Conti, because we Chinese like whatever is rare and expensive, and Bordeaux isn't anymore. We wanted Lafite because we thought it was the most precious thing in the world. Now we know that's Romanée-Conti, and we can get Lafite whenever we want it."[7]

Wei is in Beaune to be trained as an official Burgundy wine spokesperson for China. With a few other participants, he religiously listens to Jean-Pierre Renard, an instructor at the Burgundy wine school, who is supposed to teach them the basics of Burgundy climates and terroirs in a single week. Renard finds the Asian enthusiasm for his region amusing. "The Chinese all want to taste Romanée-Conti, and when I tell them it's impossible, they literally follow me around saying they're ready to put a million euros on the table and that I can keep five hundred thousand for myself! It's also amusing to see how the Chinese government can be meticulous about the certificates of quality that it demands of our wines, and, all of a sudden, extremely indulgent when it's about bringing in bottles of our finest wines," the instructor says ironically. "Our exporters will tell you every part of the government machinery gets its case of wine. It's not corruption; it's services rendered."[8]

The Burgundy wine industry is clever and has turned its weakness into an advantage. "We make very small volumes. The problem in Burgundy isn't how to sell our wine, as it is in Bordeaux, but how to have enough of it to satisfy our clients,"[9] observes Nelly Blau-Picard, the head of exports for the Burgundy wine industry association. Managing this scarcity means making prices go up while at the same time carefully avoiding getting onto terrain that's too speculative. "Some certainly would have done it with great pleasure. Sell everything to the Chinese, make the prices go up. Except that Burgundy is two thousand eight hundred producers and two hundred fifty merchants. Even if we wanted to move heaven and earth for China, to make everyone change at once is tougher than in Bordeaux." Plus, they've kept their farmer mentality in Burgundy, and they won't put all their eggs in one basket. It's just common sense. When the Chinese came and asked them to drop their regular clientele, most of the winemakers said no.

They certainly had good intuition. But these vague attempts at resistance didn't stop the finest estates in this beautiful region from also being drawn into the madness of skyrocketing prices. The New Zealand website wine-searcher.com put prestigious Burgundy wines at the top of its list of the top fifty most expensive wines in the world—far ahead of the top Bordeaux.

13

VINO CHINA

A true revolution has been happening over the last two decades. Wine has been thrust from the nineteenth century into the twenty-first. Sales are brisk, and prices have peaked. Over twenty years, the amount of land sold has doubled and the price per hectare has increased by a factor of three,[1] or even a factor of ten or fifteen in certain prestigious appellations. In just a few years, the French wine industry has become a pie that foreign investors are eager to get a piece of.

Buyers are ready to buy almost anything, at any price. There is so much excitement that Christie's auction house recently opened Vineyards by Christie's International Real Estate in Hong Kong, a department entirely devoted to wealthy foreigners eager to buy the most prestigious vineyards in the world. These buyers can now count on the connections and the discretion of the best specialists. Sales aren't about to slow down anytime soon.

Even if the local residents are upset, it seems quite difficult to resist this siren song from afar, and the desire for riches. The châteaux sold to the Chinese go for prices well above the market value. Last year, all of Burgundy was stirred up at the news of the sale of the Château of Gevrey-Chambertin. The landmark building, built between the eleventh and thirteenth centuries, and its 2 hectares of vineyards were sold to a casino owner from Macao for €8 million. Naturally, the wine syndicate hadn't sat idly by. It was even ready to offer €4 or €5 million, although the appraisals weren't above €3.5 million. But with an Asian investor ready to pay €8 million, any moral dilemmas the sellers may have had vanished.

Bordeaux is used to this kind of thing. In 1997, the Hong Kong banker Peter Kwok bought Château Haut-Brisson in Saint-Émilion, and he went on to purchase Tour Saint-Christophe (Saint-Émilion) and La Patache (Pomerol)—a château for each of his three children. Since then, many more real estate transactions have taken place.

While the pace was slow until 2011 (one or two per year), it has now reached a mad speed: fifteen transactions in 2011, and twenty-seven in 2012. How can anyone resist buyers prepared to spend €10 million to €30 million for estates that aren't even the best? The industry did tremble to see the *grand cru* Bellefont-Belcier fall into Chinese hands. An iron ore magnate, one Mr. Wang, bought this jewel in Saint-Émilion that covers 20 hectares, 13 of them contiguous. Again, the price was staggering: €1 to €2 million per hectare, or about €40 million total. The shrewd Mr. Wang did wait to purchase until the château obtained its *grand cru* classification, which, of course, it did.

"These are complicated people. There's no direction, and we don't really know where they're going and what they're doing. A hundred percent of the wine goes to China and we don't see it anymore. It's like an abduction,"[2] regrets Hubert de Boüard. In fact, it's estimated today that with the 1,000 hectares of French vineyards that they've purchased, the Chinese send about 8 million bottles directly to the Chinese market with no French intermediaries.

Not to mention that once they're in China, these millions of bottles of French wine from vineyards less scrupulously run than Mr. Wang's sometimes multiply through the magic of adding some Argentine wine. "When I hear people in Bordeaux say it's great that 'our Chinese friends' are buying estates here, I know that many of them totally misunderstand the market,"[3] observes Stéphane Derenoncourt. "Some Chinese who buy estates here do it only for the label. Once they have the brand, they register it there and bring in shipping containers of South American wine that they sell as Bordeaux. This whole Asian windfall has made us a bit nuts."

"You can't stop the Chinese from wanting to do business,"[4] smiles the gentlemanly Peter Kwok. He asks for a little understanding for these newcomers. "When they see the price of wine here, and the price that they buy it for over there, they can't help but be tempted to get into this business."[5] But these purchases gradually educate the Chinese consumer. As for the investors, they are starting to want to make fine wines that they can also sell on the French market.

Peter Kwok, who was the first Chinese buyer of Bordeaux vineyards, decided to sell on the *en primeur* market this year.[6] He wants his wines to reach great heights and to stop being considered Chinese wines for the Chinese market. But even he acknowledges that every year before this one, he sent all his Saint-Émilion to China because it was not good enough for French connoisseurs. "Now it's good, and I aspire to something more, especially—why not?—to have my wines classified in 2022."[7]

Peter Kwok is a pragmatic businessman. He unemotionally describes the various kinds of Asian Bordeaux vineyard buyers. "There are those who want to make a killing by selling the wine they make here for a good price; there are those who see that for the price of an apartment in Hong Kong, they can get a château in France . . . And, of course, there are also some bad boys,"[8] he admits. That's a euphemism for all those investors who came to French soil for unseemly reasons.

In its most recent report, Tracfin, the French government office that fights money laundering, criticized all the strange transactions that have taken place in French wine country. It condemned the purchase of properties with significant operational deficits, which thus allows dirty money to be laundered in secret, using "complex financial and legal dealings by a series of companies established in countries with favorable taxation policies."[9]

"It was about time that Tracfin do something," says Dominique Techer. "In 1998, when I was mayor of Pomerol,

I contacted them about strange transactions. I was told then that these were respectable entities . . . Ultimately they can't just ignore this stuff, if these watchdogs are going to have any credibility or usefulness."[10]

The complexity of these financial deals surely explains the very low profile of Chinese wine investors. None of them wants to speak or appear in the media. A winemaker was strongly reprimanded for having dared to suggest bringing someone along to his first meeting with an important Chinese businessman. The Canadian manager setting up the meeting with the investor dashed off a threatening e-mail intimating that he should keep both the project and the individual buyer completely confidential. He would later learn that all the businessman's collaborators are required to sign a confidentiality agreement that forbids them from publicly identifying him by name.

Meanwhile, in Bordeaux, tension is mounting and a dormant racism is rearing its head. Sandrine Bosc, who just left the general management of Peter Kwok's vineyards, complained about certain remarks that winemakers made to her when she was still working for a "yellow man." This palpable tension burst out when young Chinese oenology students were assaulted at the last Vinexpo. While totally unacceptable, such behavior still highlights a real discomfort.

"Without slipping into reactionary protectionism, we should be careful not to let our vineyards turn into Chinatown and not to endanger our land's delicate balance in exchange for chimerical dreams of riches,"[11] warns Stéphane Derenoncourt.

It's far from certain that these commonsense arguments will stand up against the voracious appetites of owners looking for a big sale. As long as this bubble doesn't burst, it's hard to believe that wine producers will turn away the purchasers that have huge buying power.

14

THE SHARKS DIVIDE UP
THE LAND

This is the story of a rich heiress, the daughter of a Gaullist politician who thought she would be welcomed as a savior on her family lands in the Bordeaux region but who realized bitterly that the local sharks saw her as defenseless prey to be swallowed in one gulp.

Aline Guichard-Goldschmidt, the daughter of Olivier Guichard, decided to run the manor of Siaurac and its vineyards after her father's death in January 2004.

She wanted to give her husband the rural roots he had always dreamed of. She wanted to revive this splendid house inherited from her adored grandmother Baroness Guichard and her grandfather Louis, the former chief of staff of Admiral Darlan. He was a complicated but loving man, whom Olivier never stopped defining himself against.

Aline knew that her two older sisters, Constance Poniatowski, managing editor of *Version Femina*, and publisher Malcy Ozannat, wanted to sell and that it would be difficult to settle the estate. No matter, she held firm and, with a convert's fervor, threw herself fully into the world of wine. She was convinced she'd be welcomed with open arms by her colleagues and neighbors: "I was sure the small world of Bordeaux would be thrilled that our estate didn't fall into the hands of some insurance company or industrialist but remained a family business."[1]

"It's true that the vultures are feasting around here,"[2] says Dominique Techer ironically. Construction and real estate magnate Martin Bouygues reigns over Saint-Estèphe, LVMH CEO Bernard Arnault continues to expand his fabulous kingdom (Cheval Blanc, Yquem, Krug, Ruinart . . .), and insurance companies such as AG2R La Mondiale gobble up whatever the other billionaires leave behind.

"I thought people would be grateful to me for leaving my life in Paris and my husband's very comfortable salary to come back to the estate. Instead, I'm threatened, vilified, and despised. These people are fighting a feudal war from the pages of history against me,"[3] Aline says, outraged. Whether they're French or foreign, the big guns respect one another. Attracted by the appetizing scent of fresh meat, they are not at all as open-minded as people usually think.

But Aline didn't realize any of this in the beginning.

First, she had to settle the inheritance issue with her sisters, which was complicated because the estate was so large. In addition to the manor and its land, there were the 46 hectares of Lalande-de-Pomerol, the 6 hectares of Saint-Émilion *grand cru classé*, and especially the 3.67 hectares of

Vray Croix de Gay located on the prestigious Pomerol plateau, behind Pétrus. The markets for the wine were guaranteed because Christian Moueix—whose family is the seventh biggest wine fortune in France according to the June 2013 list in the magazine *Challenges*—was in charge of it.

Christian Moueix is the son of Jean-Pierre and the brother of Jean-François. The Moueix family is a dynasty of wine merchants. Longtime Bordeaux residents like to point out, a tad scornfully, that the family is not originally from the Bordeaux region but from the department of Corrèze. Christian reigns over the Pomerol plateau and until recently handled the management of Pétrus, which belongs to his brother Jean-François. After Olivier Guichard's death, Christian Moueix, who had had the exclusive right to sell his wines for twenty-five years, agreed to continue to sell 50 percent of the wine and to handle all exports. The future of Baroness Guichard's wines seemed ensured. The value of the estate was significant, especially with markets guaranteed by Christian Moueix. The bank Crédit Agricole was also there to support these enthusiastic new businesspeople and lent them "more than was reasonable."[4]

It was the beginning of an incredible drama that was part wine Western, part modern tragedy. Aline Guichard found herself owning prestigious vineyards, which Christian Moueix was very interested in, and she was greatly in debt. Back in 1998, her father, Olivier Guichard, launched a big plan to modernize his estates. The cellars were renovated and new buildings were put up. In 2001, on the advice of Christian Moueix, he hired a young manager, Yannick

Reyrel, a student of Jean-Claude Berrouet, the oenologist at Pétrus.

After all these investments, Aline Guichard expected her wines to be reevaluated by Christian Moueix. "They were sold at a fixed price and Moueix always wanted more from us, such as wooden crates . . . We just weren't making it. We asked him to raise it a few cents."[5] Surprise: Moueix refused. So Aline Guichard suggested that she sell some of her wine herself to improve her margins. She didn't ask for much: 30 percent of her wines, with Moueix retaining the export rights. Moueix magnanimously offered her 50 percent. Aline contacted other Bordeaux merchants as well as brokers to try to get better margins. They all acted interested but nothing concrete ever got decided. Then, a few days before the *en primeur* sales, a German client sent her a fax to buy allotments of her wine (options on wine that hasn't been finished yet). Aline told him that Christian Moueix handled her exports. The client answered that Christian Moueix had just sent him an e-mail saying "that he was no longer handling Baroness Guichard's wines."

Aline didn't lose her cool. She demanded an explanation from Moueix who casually told her to send him some samples so he could get an idea of the quality of her wines. He had been involved with these wines for twenty-five years and acted as if he were just discovering them! Aline sent him samples. Christian Moueix told her that the wine "was increasingly mediocre and tasted of mushrooms. But our managing oenologist had been hired by him because he had studied with the oenologist at Pétrus, which is owned by the

Moueix family."[6] For Christian, it was exclusivity or nothing at all. Then it would be nothing, Aline decided. "This was a great loss for the Jean-Pierre Moueix company,"[7] the powerful merchant says sadly, with a hypocritical tone.[8] In any case, it was his right, and he couldn't be blamed. "Except that, at the same time, the estate was settled on the basis of fifty percent sold by Moueix. We paid a high price,"[9] says Aline.

Going from total exclusivity with a big distributor to nothing at all is very risky. For one thing, the estate doesn't have any old wines to offer its clients. And who are its clients? "After twenty-five years with a merchant, you're totally at his mercy; we saw an export label come through now and then, but we had no idea who the clients were he was selling our wines to."[10] As for the other Bordeaux merchants and the brokers, none of them wanted to get on Christian Moueix's bad side. You don't look for trouble with people that powerful. Aline Guichard also realized that for many years her wine was the required punishment for those who wanted to buy Pétrus. "When your name is Moueix and you manage Pétrus with your brother, you can tell your clients, 'If you want Pétrus, you have to take Siaurac.' That happens for thirty years and it ruins the reputation of your wine. You're basically kept ignorant and then he can hope to get your land when the estate is hard to settle,"[11] says Aline Guichard. Is she jumping to conclusions? Perhaps. But this is indeed the kind of ruthlessness the wine business can lead to.

This charming, polite woman—maybe too polite—did everything she could to make it, even hiring Alain Raynaud as a consultant to try to get a good score from Parker.

Alas, the value of Baroness Guichard's wine is very low, as are her finances. Strangely enough, Crédit Agricole, which previously had been extremely easygoing, suddenly became insistent about seizing the accounts. "Since we were really in a tight spot, Crédit Agricole said to us, casually, 'You should just sell some properties—Pomerol, for example.'"[12] The appellation where Christian Moueix reigns, since he owns about ten of the approximately 150 properties there and sells half the Pomerol wine that is produced.

Financially squeezed and truly desperate, Aline Guichard will have to fight this battle on another front.

15

The Long March
of the Pomerol Exiles

On the sublime soil of our greatest vineyards, behind the
golden gates of these beautiful châteaux, Shakespearean tragedies play out every day. These wine-country sharks are like
the feudal lords of old. Their daily battle is to increase their
territory at any cost. Too bad for the little people who find
themselves in their way. They are the prey the sharks won't
hesitate to swallow, very cheaply if at all possible.

The sharks recently decided that it was time to get
rid of the peasants on the prestigious Pomerol plateau. To
do this, they relied on the usual strategies. The first one is
always to get hold of the wine syndicate. It's especially easy
since the Pomerol wine syndicate, like the others, has rees-
tablished voting by property ownership: the more hectares
and properties you own, the more votes you have. Next,
they just had to get the trick approved by the wine industry
watchdog the INAO. So all they needed was an excuse to
get rid of the people in their way. In 2009, the syndicate

leaders finally found the thing they needed: requiring all the Pomerol producers to build a wine aging cellar within the Pomerol region.

For many, this new requirement, approved by order of the INAO (and signed by the minister at the time, Bruno Le Maire), is impossible to fulfill. Winemakers with very small plots of land simply don't have room to build a cellar. Plus, even if they had the space, they don't have the money. Requiring these winemakers to build a cellar means forcing them to invest around €500,000, money that most of them don't have.

It's a cruel blow, especially since, for decades, these winegrowers, and their parents and grandparents before them, made their Pomerol wine a few kilometers outside the appellation area without it bothering anyone. Casting tradition aside, the syndicate suddenly decided that this practice was extremely harmful to the quality of the wine, and thus to Pomerol's reputation. Twenty-three properties out of the appellation's 150 found themselves excluded. In its great mercy, the INAO granted them the possibility of continuing to make their wine until 2018. That would give the sharks time to make offers on the properties. Until then, the exiles (a term the syndicate's president Jean-Marie Garde rejects, claiming they're all part of the same family)[1] can fight and make their case, although in the meantime, as benevolent future buyers kindly explained to them, "the closer they came to the fateful date, the more their land would lose value." For just before the harvest in 2018, the winemakers would have only one option left: to sell at whatever price the sharks offered.

The exiles moved heaven and earth to try to put a stop to this decree. First, they turned to their syndicate, hoping it was simply a misunderstanding. When they contacted Jean-Marie Garde, who was also general secretary of the Interprofessional Council of Bordeaux Wines, he preferred to let Christian Moueix handle the matter. He's one of the most important wine producers in Pomerol and, naturally, an influential member of the syndicate's board. He warned the exiles: "If we hold a new vote, there will again be a majority."[2] Among these nobodies, there are several small vineyard owners whose wine is sold exclusively or wholesale by Moueix. Most of them thus have no interest in getting on the bad side of their only client.

Nine brave souls out of the twenty-three exiles decided to fight back anyway. And they won their appeal to the Council of State, France's supreme administrative court, on March 9, 2012! The INAO decree, signed by minister Bruno Le Maire, was struck down for overreaching its authority. In its decision, the Council of State expressed astonishment at the motivation of the agriculture minister and the INAO, who justified this new measure "by the necessity of limiting the transportation and handling of wine in order to preserve its quality." But the grapes are being transported, not the wine. Moreover, as the court pointed out, "Some wine producers transport their harvest within the geographical production area over distances that can be greater than those over which the plaintiffs transport their harvest."[3] The Council of State also questioned the drastic elimination of any proximity zone, with the noticeable exception of two plots of land that were conveniently allowed because their owners were in the old-boy network. Basically, they wanted to kick out a few winemakers in favor of many others, and it was a bit too obvious.

Anticipating that their decree would be rejected, the syndicate and the INAO immediately came up with another one, which, in its great clemency, gave the exiles three more years to get into line. In the first decree, they had forbidden Pomerol winemakers from making their wine in neighboring villages outside the region because it apparently harmed the quality of the wines. Now, in the second version, they stated that Pomerol wine could be made not just in Pomerol but also in the town of Libourne, where many big merchants have their warehouses. You see, the old traditional proximity zones seriously harm the quality of Pomerol, but it seems that the Libourne warehouses must be a factor of recognized quality.[4] It's beyond absurd; it's Kafkaesque.

All these local idiosyncrasies were carefully avoided by the president of the INAO's National Committee for Wines, who, when asked about this inconvenient case, gave the incredible reply, "Don't ask!"[5] The excuse? Insufficient knowledge of the case, it seems. It's too much. Christian Paly admits that situations like this are emerging all over France, especially in the most prestigious appellations. "In 99.99 percent of cases, there's no problem, but sometimes, purist syndicates have a very restricted view of the proximity area, which can create problems in the vicinity."[6]

That must be the explanation! Out of devotion to the quality of the wine and respect for the terroir and the taste, the Pomerol syndicate was just too meticulous. How could it be anything but that?

And here's another inconsistency: although some Pomerol vineyards no longer have the right to the appellation simply because they don't have a cellar, part of Lalande-de-Pomerol, a much less prestigious appellation, has the right, by the same decree, to call itself Pomerol. INAO and the syndicate took care to add an appendix to settle this little matter. So the Château de Sales vineyard in Lalande makes Pomerol wine! This goes back to a Bordeaux civil court decision of December 29, 1928. Basically, it had been the custom in the region for decades—like the proximity zone of vineyards without cellars? Yes, but this time, it concerns a friend, so it's a bit different. The Château de Sales belongs to Bruno de Lambert, the vice president of the syndicate, the organization that supervised the writing of the decrees. When asked about this exception, the vice president took it very badly.[7]

The exiles decided to keep on fighting, but an important member of their ranks dropped out: Jean-Louis Trocard, former president of the Interprofessional Council of Bordeaux Wines (CIVB). In the meantime, by pure chance, of course, his son had had a stroke of luck. INAO allowed the Libourne racetrack, which was purportedly dilapidated, to be turned into a little over 13 hectares of grapevines in the Pomerol appellation. A racetrack! With real estate prices in Pomerol being what they are, this opportune transformation of a horse racing facility into a noble terroir was a lucky break. Especially in an appellation where every piece of land for sale attracts intense interest. And Benoît Trocard, the son of Jean-Louis, was conveniently able to get 2.08 hectares—2 hectares sold at the bargain price of €446,000 per hectare[8] (a hectare sells for €1 million in that part of the appellation), which were worth a little understanding toward the syndicate. Jean-Louis Trocard maintains that he supports his former colleagues on the substance of the issue but admits that the "possibility" offered to his son to expand resulted in a "change in strategy"[9] that led him to decide not to continue the lawsuit with his colleagues. It's carefully worded, but the meaning is very clear.

As for the INAO, it wants to remind us of the noble missions of this great organization. Isn't one of them, according to its president Christian Paly, "to have a structuring role in land-use planning in order to prevent certain parts of France from remaining in distress?"[10]

The lucrative ennoblement of land formerly devoted to the pleasures of horse racing surely is part of this sacred duty.

While waiting for the land to be divided and the wolves to be satisfied, Aline Guichard, drowning in debt, is bravely determined to keep her 3 hectares on the Pomerol plateau—3 hectares that risk losing their value as the fateful date of 2021 approaches.[11]

But Christian Moueix, always considerate, regularly informs the Guichard family that he will always be there when they're in need. He also sent them a letter[12] assuring them that he was ready, in his great clemency, to make a cellar available to them so that they would no longer suffer from the syndicate's decision. "It's in spirit of 'reconciliation' that I suggested in my letter of December 15, 2011, that they rent a small fermenting room and the cellar of a property that we had just acquired and didn't need for immediate use. I never got an answer,"[13] emphasizes the generous merchant. In a twist of fate, this letter was used against the exiles in the case they brought to the Council of State. Not very fraternal behavior on the powerful landowner's part? Yet he claims to have only one desire: a community truce in his appellation. He even told me that he hoped "your writings will contribute to peace in Pomerol."[14]

Thus, when Christian Moueix asked once again to visit her, just a friendly visit between neighbors (Christian had just bought some land not far from Aline's property), the baroness decided to cover herself by asking for a letter from his lawyer attesting that this meeting could in no way be inserted into any legal proceedings.

He still had the meeting. He came and made light-hearted conversation about harmless topics and presented the baroness with six bottles of La Fleur-Pétrus. Like an offering to his future prey.

Since then, Aline is trembling in her boots. The wolf is at the door: does he know that she had a bad year and that a possible sale looks more likely? More critically does he know just how determined the baroness is?

Her tenacity has paid off, because she has once more prevailed in court: the Council of State[15] has just rejected, yet again, the INAO's latest decree on the definition of the proximity zone in Pomerol's quality charter. It is a sigh of relief for her and her colleagues, but she's only partly reassured. She knows the local lords only too well and is sure they won't give up so easily. Nevertheless, she's energized by this victory and more ready than ever to keep up the fight. She'll need all her strength. The sharks have already found a charade to get rid of the little guys.[16] They told Aline about it on December 24. No Christmas holiday in the enchanted kingdom.

16

You Have to
Think Bigger

Through the intermediary of the professional associations, at least in Bordeaux, winemakers have the power to create vineyards out of thin air, excluding anyone who gets in their way. But are land wars unique to this area? What is it like elsewhere, in other prestigious wine regions? A trip to Champagne suddenly puts the power of the Pomerol elite into perspective. For all these little Bordeaux dramas are only trifles compared to the fratricidal war Champagne residents are fighting to expand their appellation.

This wonderful Champagne tradition was starting to feel a bit confined. It had sold so well to celebrate the year 2000, expansion was imperative. They'd already done miracles in planting everywhere they could, and even beyond. In a November 2010 letter, the local wine syndicate recalled that "in the '70s, grapes were planted on about 17,000 hectares" and emphasized that there remained "15,000 hectares of vineyards still to be planted."[1] Forty years later, the area has doubled and, according to the local authorities, it's still not enough. Since a field planted with Champagne grapes is worth about two hundred times the same field planted with wheat, everyone is extremely interested in turning lead into gold.

As a result, all the towns that couldn't claim part of this gold mine fought to be included in the appellation area. With so much money at stake, naturally lawsuits multiplied. The syndicate and the INAO ended up taking the bull by the horns. In 2003, the general syndicate of Champagne winemakers (SGV) had its members vote on the following resolution: "Do you give the syndicate in defense of the appellation the task of organizing, together with the INAO, a review of the geographical area and criteria that define the Champagne region?" Unsurprisingly, the yeses won, with 393 votes out of 418. But everyone is still waiting for the review to happen, and with independent experts expressing different opinions, the time frame keeps getting pushed back.

"This'll be worse than the scramble for Africa," jokes Bertrand Auboyneau, owner of the bistro Paul Bert and a knowledgeable observer of the Champagne region. "The interests are so huge."[2] A parallel market has come into being, where lands are bought and sold well above their objective value in the hope they'll become part of the Champagne appellation. "These guys have gone crazy; they'd kill their mother and father to get land though they don't even know what it will ultimately be worth,"[3] explains a consultant who is a member of the independent winemakers' syndicate. No one wants to speak publicly about this issue. Everyone cites some sordid event to explain his or her silence. So-and-so was shot to death in such and such a town that will supposedly become part of the Champagne AOC. Rumors and fantasies run wild.

"I don't want to die over this. Money makes people crazy. They've all become speculators here," says a worried winemaker in the Aube department. Jean-Sébastien Fleury, a landowner in Côte des Bar, isn't very optimistic either about this land war whose outcome is still very uncertain: "We won't see the effects of the INAO's reform until 2018 to 2019. And that's only if the reform goes well. It's not starting off well. Some areas may be declassified and reclassified. The winemakers who get declassified will definitely appeal. It's a very delicate issue and the wine professionals can't guarantee any particular time frame and don't want to say anything."[4]

Starting in the late nineties, the syndicate had asked one of its former presidents to engage in preliminary identification of plots of land for this future classification that may happen in 2020. "Oddly enough, a certain number of elected officials at the time ended up with AOC lands in villages where they didn't even have a garden before!" says one winemaker. "They assure us of the fairness of the classification and the integrity of these independent experts, but I doubt it."[5] It's true that our wine-making friends aren't very good at independent expertise. Some Champagne residents were disturbed to see that one of the former presidents of the general syndicate of Champagne winemakers, which is very involved in the reclassification issue, was chosen as an independent expert on the commission for the Saint-Émilion classification. "You can be sure that one of these days one of his pals from Bordeaux will show up and conveniently reclassify lands in Champagne, totally independently . . . It's quid pro quo with those people!"[6]

Those who are suspicious may not be entirely wrong. In fact, the head of the INAO's wine committee is leaning toward "putting together an 'independent' investigative commission made up of people outside the geographical area in question."[7] For him, this is the only way "to handle this thorny issue with huge financial stakes completely impartially."[8]

Having been burned by their Bordeaux adventures and aware that their reputation is at stake here—or at least whatever is left of it—the INAO's apparatchiks "are now moving forward cautiously and thoughtfully."[9]

Basically, the message is: you need to wait.

In any case, even before the revision of the AOC area, this region has always seen harsh infighting. Each piece of land that's sold is the object of fierce battles. The Beauforts learned this the hard way. This family stands out in this very polished milieu. The father, Jacques, has grown his grapes organically since 1971, which takes serious commitment when you're in Ambonnay, in the Marne department, on the best Champagne lands, the area where all the most prestigious companies have their estates. But he's very religious and sees his conversion to organic winegrowing like Paul's on the road to Damascus. His sons settled in Polisy, in the Aube department, buying a château that was in ruins after a fire. "People from Marne are not at all liked in Aube,"[10] observes Bertrand Gautherot, a brave winemaker who was kicked out of his cooperative for having dared to go organic. "It's a very old rivalry; our land is considered much less noble than Marne. Meanwhile, we have twenty-two percent of the Champagne area, but we only make five percent of the champagne. People in Marne buy our grapes. That's how it works."[11] So, when the Beaufort sons left Marne for Polisy and bought the château, there was an outcry. "They certainly weren't popular, and plus they have ten kids and they're organic!"[12] laughs Bertrand. The Beauforts aren't the type to be so easily discouraged. They bought the land, made it profitable, and even tried to buy more, but they were rejected. By whom? The local real estate and rural planning agency (SAFER) and the wine-making syndicate. SAFER is supposed to protect farmland and support young farmers. The Beauforts are young farmers. This was in the early 2000s, when the price of land in Champagne was high but hadn't yet skyrocketed, and Joachim got used to "buying a plot of land every year by taking out reasonable loans."[13] He purchased two plots of land with no problem, but then his land "appetite" started to upset the nearby big companies. SAFER solved the problem by preempting his purchase. What does that mean? Let's look at SAFER's description. This noble institution explains that "according to articles L 143-1 and L 143-2 of the rural code, the law gives it the option of using a right of preemption . . . SAFER agencies are systematically informed by lawyers of planned sales and they can take the place of the original buyer, their goal being to resell to another buyer whose plans better correspond to local planning needs." And this is "always in the goal of the general interest."[14] Joachim Beaufort must have really been harming the general interest, and his father's forty years of organic winegrowing must not have made him the ideal candidate for "protecting the environment," since he didn't get to buy the land. "My brother was buying as a young farmer," explains Joachim's brother Quentin. "The land was sold to a young man who lives in Montgueux, almost fifty kilometers from here, even though one of SAFER's primary missions is to avoid the dispersal of lands."[15] Why that young man? It must have been a coincidence, but that young man was under contract with one of the Champagne magnates, Paul-François Vranken,[16] to whom he sold his grapes. No one doubts that Vranken must have had urgent need for an additional hectare of land. Vranken Pommery Monopole is the second-biggest company in Champagne[17] after LVMH, with 10 percent of the champagne market, 20.6 million bottles, and €339.6 million in revenue. The company has access to 7,100 hectares of grapes in Champagne, Camargue, Provence, and Portugal (2,520 hectares that it owns and 4,580 hectares of grapes under contract from other winegrowers).

Starting with nothing, this man from Liège has been able to build a real empire in the space of a few decades. In Aube or Marne, no one calls him the Belgian or "what's his name" as they did at first, when he didn't yet know the customs of this small, closed-off world. From now on, he's Vranken. But his name isn't said out loud in public; it's whispered after looking around to make sure one of his men isn't nearby. In just over thirty years, this commoner has become viceroy of Champagne after Bernard Arnault and is the fifth-richest man[18] of this beautiful region, worth €226 million. But his reputation remains controversial. He did whatever it took to ensure his meteoric rise. "He brooks no opposition, and they're all under his thumb. This is a man who's used to always getting his way,"[19] says Julienne Guihard, a journalist for *L'Union* who was the first to attack his arrangements with the local landowners.

On December 16, 2009, she published an article in *L'Union* that got a lot of attention. Its title? "Scandal at the SGV [General Syndicate of Champagne Winemakers]: The Vanishing Three Million." In this article, she questioned the syndicate's very dubious purchase of a building belonging to Paul-François Vranken. The building was located at 17 Avenue de Champagne, the Champs-Élysées of Épernay. All the big companies have their offices there. In order to keep up appearances, the syndicate had to be located there, too. The deal was done in February 2003; the syndicate's board approved the transaction. The building was purchased from Vranken's company for €4.55 million—about two and a half times its value. In criticizing the incongruity of this purchase at a price that seems very inflated, Julienne Guihard relied on two estimates, one that was notarized and dated from 2006 estimating the property at €1.8 million before renovations, and another by the architect in charge of the renovation, Jean-Baptiste Michel, putting it at €1.6 million. So that's €3 million too much, not counting the millions of euros of renovations that have been sunk into the building since then.

Philippe Feneuil,[20] then president of the general syndicate of Champagne winemakers, handled the purchase. "The SGV had a lot of money in its reserves; no one asked any questions. So the board gave its OK without getting an estimate,"[21] recalls Julienne Guihard. What's €3 million between friends? But the board didn't have all the information. In particular, it was unaware of the contents of a handwritten letter dated December 6, 2002, that Philippe Feneuil sent to Paul-François Vranken. In this letter, Feneuil writes that Vranken is in agreement, "provided that SCEV (Société civile d'exploitation viticole) the Pommery use in January 2003 the plots of grapevines and vineyards requested of the departmental structures commission." "A surprising detail," observed the journalist. "Unless Philippe Feneuil could, and would, influence this commission's decision."[22] In theory, Feneuil should not have any influence over the structures commission. "This commission gives farming rights and thus avoids gross speculation and other dispossession of farmland,"[23] explains a Champagne syndicate member. "This authority will validate the fact that you can become a professional. If, to become a professional, you endanger a truck farmer who only has his two hectares to live on, this institution should logically tell you no. Paul-François Vranken is a merchant; his company is a capitalist business and not a farming company. When he bought the Pommery vineyards, he had to go through the structures commission to farm his grapevines. It could ask him to give up his land and to rent it to young people, but he wanted to get the right to farm it directly."[24]

In his letter, Feneuil also emphasizes Vranken's second requirement. He demanded to obtain "from the owners the possibility of using the outside walls . . . as well as the transfer of plots that are not classified, developed and undeveloped, equal to about 5,000 square meters."[25] Again, the journalist insists, "This new condition is curious. How does the fact whether or not Paul-François Vranken obtains or doesn't obtain the agreement of these owners concern the SGV and Philippe Feneuil? Unless, yet again, Feneuil is supposed to handle it himself, directly or indirectly."[26] All this is still not illegal but shows Vranken's influence.

This formidable businessman thus not only got over-paid by €3 million when he sold his building, but also set conditions that are even more beneficial to him. It is certainly strange that President Feneuil got his syndicate involved in a transaction that is apparently so unfavorable to it. "Especially because Feneuil was then assisted by Rolland Chaillon,[27] a former jurist and at the time the director of the SGV,"[28] Julienne Guichard says with astonishment. "The reasons for this strange transaction will surely always remain a secret among the three of them. Yet we would all love to know if there was compensation, and, if so, to whom and for what services rendered?"[29] Yet we do know that when Rolland Chaillon was dismissed by the syndicate in 2005 (after having worked there since 1979), he was immediately hired by Vranken's company. It's such a small world; this must be another coincidence.

Unsurprisingly, Mr. Vranken did not like this newspaper article. In fact, he sued the journalist for libel. Then one of the most extraordinary episodes of this whole affair took place. It happened during the filing[30] of the suit by the plaintiff and his company, Vranken-Pommery, against the newspaper *L'Union*. On February 9, 2010, the hearing was begun by the presiding judge of the criminal court in Reims, Mario-Louis Craighero.[31] He made a clerical error that could have nullified the proceedings. The newspaper's lawyers and Vranken's lawyers both noticed this. One of Vranken's lawyers went to see the clerk the next day to inform him of the error.[32] The pressure mounted on the judge, who realized that Vranken's lawyers would be dismayed if the suit could not go forward.

So the judge tried to smooth the error over with one of the newspaper's lawyers, who refused to be persuaded. Instead of getting ruffled over this detail, what did the judge do? He took out his Wite-Out and changed the small mistakes while pressuring his clerk to sign off on it! The newspaper's lawyers picked up on this trick and prepared to file suit against the judge for falsifying public records, which is a serious crime that in France can get you tried in criminal court. The judge was caught in the act, but since the suit hadn't yet been filed, he thought he still had a chance to get away with it. Sure of his connections, he decided to call on one of his contacts, a local politician named Philippe Malpezzi, a former parliamentary attaché to the center-right Union for a Popular Movement minister Renaud Dutreil, to be his go-between with Jacques Tillier, then managing editor of *L'Union*.

They met on March 11, 2010, at the Hôtel de la Paix in Reims. Tillier, who wasn't born yesterday, suspected the reasons behind this meeting. "We had it all planned out," explains Julienne Guihard. "We'd put a photographer at the door of the bar and we recorded everything." In fact, the judge presented himself as a "moderating" influence at the court regarding the newspaper and asked Jacques Tillier to calm his lawyer down. Basically: do me this favor, let's forget about this whole business and *L'Union* will never have any more legal problems. Not satisfied with having falsified documents, the judge compromised himself in a shady affair of passive corruption. Of course, the newspaper's lawyers went ahead and filed suit against the judge. Craighero, judged by his peers, got one of the worst punishments: compulsory retirement. But, once again, the crux of the matter is missing. Why did the judge take such risks to please Paul-François Vranken? He knew full well he was risking his career. The national division of financial investigations in Nanterre, which looked into the case, also regretted that the investigation was not continued. "Indeed, there is still no guarantee that Mr. Craighero wasn't paid for his actions and that he has no direct or indirect connection with Mr. Vranken of the Vranken-Pommery-Monopole company for whom the original decision was prejudicial, which their lawyers pointed out to Mr. Craighero."[33]

This lawsuit must have been particularly important to the local magnate because, when his own lawsuit was frozen by the Craighero case, President Feneuil decided, although it was late in the game, to sue the newspaper and the journalist himself. Feneuil didn't win the case, and during the proceedings he even had to explain the envelopes of cash that he got from his syndicate when he was president. "It's true that it's not good for the tax authorities,"[34] he stammered during the proceedings, although he didn't explain what the money was for.

So, when Paul-François Vranken wants something, everyone—or almost everyone—jumps to it.

Here, too, the financial stakes are massive. Vranken spent €152 million to buy the Pommery brand, the Reims site, about 20 hectares of vineyards, the cellars, the reserves, and the supply contracts from LVMH in 2002. But not most of the Pommery grapes. The 470 hectares of grapevines, including 300 located in the best Champagne vintages,[35] remain in the hands of Bernard Arnault. Would it be a dumb question to ask how Vranken manages to keep the Pommery taste without the Pommery grapes? All the professionals in the region whisper about this mystery, but none of them has yet managed to solve it.

All these big brands must not need the grapes or the terroir to create fine wine. Their amazing skill must be enough.

17

THE HELICOPTERS OF
GOOD TASTE

Jacques Beaufort, a winemaker in Ambonnay in the Marne department, whose son Joachim had to battle the local lords for land, is quite a character. A fervent Catholic, he sees his winegrowing as a true calling. But for years he suffered because of allergies that affected him every time a helicopter spraying pesticides flew over his land.

He was mocked and considered the local eccentric. Imagine: Jacques practices organic wine making! This choice seems utopian in Champagne, especially in the Marne department, where every bit of land is planted all the way to the road and the vines are as close together as humanly possible. He's not at all the combative type, and he went to speak to each of his neighbors, explaining his health problems over and over again. But instead of finding an attentive ear, the winemaker encountered only sarcastic smirks. Without exception, they all turned their backs on him because he wanted them to stop spraying chemicals everywhere. His own organic farming was one thing, but they weren't going to stand for any activism on his part. Unwell and banished from his community, he was at the end of his rope. "Starting in March, I'd get allergies. These guys treated their land until July. I was desperate. I went into the vineyard on rainy days thinking I'd feel better. It was worse. The doctor said I should put on gloves. But I couldn't prune with them on. I tried to work things out with my neighbors. I even went to see the prefect. No results."[1]

Then, one day, it was just too much. One of his neighbors looked him right in the eye and said, "'If you had any balls, Beaufort, you would've taken us to court already.' I filed the suit right afterward."[2] On February 17, 1988, in decision number 185, the Reims civil court of appeals found in his favor against Coop Air. The helicopters would no longer fly over his land.

He paid dearly for this victory. He endured repeated harassment: someone "accidentally" contaminated some of his grapevines, someone "forgot" to turn the pesticide spray off when going by his fields, etc. But it would take more than that to stop this rebellious winemaker.

Fortunately, these brave winegrowers are now protected by legislation and will no longer have to fight for their health. Ever since the 2010 Grenelle II Act, crop dusters no longer have the right to fly over our countryside. But the lawmakers wisely left a loophole. The helicopters are banned, but there are exemptions. Things worked out nicely for the landowners: for the last two years, considering the staggering number of decrees issued by the prefectures, they didn't waste any time making sure the helicopters could continue spraying at their leisure. In 2012, three towns in the Aube department and 154 towns in the Marne department (out of the 635 in the entire Champagne appellation) got a pass to spread toxic products through the air. Seventy-six advance declarations were filed before July 1, 2012.[3] In 2013, it started up again, on 350 hectares. In Burgundy, in 2012, six decrees were issued affecting over one hundred towns including Pommard, Gevrey-Chambertin, Meursault, Chambolle-Musigny, Chablis, Saint-Aubin, etc. In 2013, over 400 hectares were sprayed in Saône-et-Loire and 1,100 in Côte-d'Or.[4]

This clemency on the part of the authorities is surprising, especially considering how controversial crop dusting is. The chemicals only rarely hit their target. According to a joint study by the National Center for Agricultural Mechanization, Rural Engineering, Rivers, and Forests (CEMAGREF)[5] and the National Institute for Agronomic Research (INRA), dispersal into the environment is always more significant with aerial spraying,[6] and in winegrowing it reaches 70 percent to 95 percent.[7]

In regions like Champagne that love their helicopters, scientists have found a cocktail of banned chemicals[8] in the air, as well as folpel,[9] a fungicide suspected of causing cancer.[10] Significant doses of this toxic substance were floating in the atmosphere.[11] Yet these researchers' discoveries were limited by inadequate technology. It was impossible for them to detect mancozeb, a frequently used fungicide that is suspected of being an endocrine disruptor, meaning that it produces harmful effects on fetal development during pregnancy.[12] One thing's for sure: when the helicopter goes by, you'd better stay indoors.

The helicopters are supposed to observe a safety distance of fifty meters, but researchers admit that this distance is ridiculously low and certainly not enough to protect residents. Even if the law had stipulated one hundred meters, it would still be inadequate.[13] The scientific report by INERIS (National Institute for the Industrial Environment and Risks) is very clear: "Across all situations, at fifty meters . . . the risk is acceptable (given traditionally accepted reference values) in only 35% to 50% of cases according to the organism, while it is acceptable in only 45% to 60% of cases at a distance of one hundred meters. We observe that increasing the 'safety' distance from fifty to one hundred meters does not constitute significantly more effective protection for the wildlife being considered."

Given this data, there should easily be a consensus to ban aerial spraying. But the wine-making press constantly castigates "media who don't understand anything about agriculture,"[14] who in their ignorance celebrated the banning of the helicopters. Not enough pesticides are allowed; not enough exemptions are given: the cries of the pro-pesticide side are heartbreaking! In an editorial,[15] Bertrand Collard, the editor in chief of La Vigne, bitterly regrets that "chemical products, and even the simple fact of spraying the vines, [are] criticized with rising frequency. People don't see the services they provide, only the problems they cause." And in the same issue,[16] La Vigne wrote about a news item that revealed the "bad mind-set" of public opinion and local officials. The magazine was disturbed that Claude Paudière, mayor of Saulchery, in the Aisne department, issued a decree on March 12, 2012, forbidding winegrowers to spray two plots of land located right next to the school during school hours, i.e., between 8:20 and 11:40 a.m. and 1:20 and 4:40 p.m., so that the schoolchildren wouldn't be exposed to pesticides. "A commonsense decree," the mayor explains, "that never would have been necessary if a winegrower hadn't massively sprayed a field next to the school during recess." But the winemakers' syndicate didn't see it that way, calling these "excessive measures" and arguing that "a four-meter-high wall separates the schoolyard from the field." What if this decree opened the door to requests from residents who don't want to be showered with pesticides when they go out of their houses? Unthinkable.

To hear the syndicates tell it, all possible precautions are taken to protect local residents. Take the example of the helicopter. The town hall must be informed forty-eight hours before spraying.[17] Right afterward, a municipal employee will post the authorization to spray. This means that if, by chance, you happen to walk in front of the town hall that day, and if your eyes miraculously fall on a bunch of notices haphazardly tacked to a board, you'll be informed. So you can't say we didn't warn you. And since information circulates perfectly, we don't know how to explain the fact that in a pretty town in the Aube department a teacher on a field trip with her entire class was soaked in pesticides. Or how a man behind the wheel of his splendid Bentley convertible was sprayed. "Some days, you want to throw a shovel at the helicopter,"[18] rails a winemaker. "And they don't do it halfway. The pilot passes by once and waves, and that means, pack your bags and beat it! Because the second time he comes by, you really don't want to be out there."[19] For the organic winemakers, the helicopters are a curse: in 2005, in the Aube department, many winemakers saw their grapes lose organic certification because they had been sprayed with chemicals. It's not easy to grow organic grapes with helicopters overhead.

Meanwhile, an important ruling was handed down in criminal court. A fifty-seven-year-old farmer named Francisco Parra and his partner, a fifty-four-year-old pilot named Eduardo Pancell, were both found guilty "of having polluted the environment."[20] They got a suspended sentence of three years in prison for using polluting pesticides suspected of causing birth defects and cancer. A severe punishment. However, this ruling came from a court not in France but in Argentina. At least some other countries are taking the threat of pesticides seriously.

18

LITTLE ARRANGEMENTS
BETWEEN LORDS

Meanwhile, in Saint-Émilion, the outlook is good, at least for the elite. Since the blessing of the bells of Angélus—a celestial offering to the divine authorities who smiled upon all the *grands crus* crowned by the most recent classification—the atmosphere is peaceful. Many critics of this strange competition thought it was nothing short of miraculous. Winemaker Dominique Técher[1] was amazed by "the transformation of the modest terroir of Château Quinault L'Enclos into a *grand cru classé*." This château belonged to Robert Parker's "friend" Alain Raynaud until 2008, when Raynaud sold it to Bernard Arnault and Albert Frère.

All those who know the milieu well think it's funny to see the sands of Saint-Émilion, meaning the modest terroirs of the appellation, elevated to the ranks of *grands crus classés*. "All 750 vintages of the appellation could claim classification because terroir is no longer a required factor!"[2] cries Franck

Dubourdieu, a former Bordeaux merchant who is now at war against what he calls an invasion of globalized taste.

"We have centuries of wine making behind us, which means that all the mistakes have already been made. But that didn't stop the people behind this classification from making more!" says a winemaker who owns one of the most prestigious estates in the world. "They rewrote history by classifying terroirs that are known for making very mediocre wines. They considered the terroir good because the coach was good, but this is like performance-enhancing drugs," rails this expert. He privately mocks the fact that in Bordeaux, a land of *vins de garde* that should be aged for years, the classification standards took into account only the last ten or fifteen vintages. "*Grands crus* like a 1999 Ausone are only now ready to drink. On the other hand, all the modern, gussied-up wines that were victorious in this classification age very quickly. It's very rare to see wines from the plains [i.e., modest terroirs] age for fifty years." And this angry expert concludes by comparing the classification to a beauty contest: "There's as much difference between the first classification and today's as between a beauty contest in the fifties and one today. The winners are all remodeled, full of silicone, and extravagantly made up. That's what the beauty of the wines certified by the INAO is like."

"With rare exceptions, this new promotion favors the powerful: investors who came from elsewhere to this paradise of red gold and everyone who tries their hardest to please critics in marathon tastings instead of lovers of fine wine,"[3] laments Franck Dubourdieu.

But these disputes over taste conceal the real issue: big money. Beneath the controversy and invectives against the liberties taken regarding history and terroir lie the true reasons for this bitter war. For, in a masterful tour de force, this is the most fabulous real estate heist—metaphorically speaking, of course—that Bordeaux has ever seen. Behind the Quinault L'Enclos miracle and the vehement protests of wine lovers who criticize a taste heresy was a deal that was smoothly executed by Albert Frère and Bernard Arnault for a château whose market value has skyrocketed. And there were lots of Bernard Arnaults during the last version of the classification.

"We went from eight hundred hectares of *grands crus classés* in 1996—sixteen percent of the fifty-five hundred hectares of the AOC—to thirteen hundred hectares in 2012—twenty-four percent,"[4] Franck Dubourdieu points out. Since becoming a *grand cru classé* increases land prices by a factor of three or four, this is a profitable development. "Between three hundred and five hundred million euros of land value was given away,"[5] estimates the anonymous owner of a prestigious Saint-Émilion château.

In other words, the winners have hit the jackpot. Jean-Luc Thunevin admits as much and is happy to finally see a way out of debt: "In terms of real estate, we'll gain enormously. The *premiers crus* are at over three million euros per hectare."[6] As for Jean-François Quenin, president of the winemakers' syndicate, he goes all over Saint-Émilion saying that his property is now worth in euros the amount he paid in francs, ten times as much.

The excellent Hubert de Boüard won't lose out either, since, according to the magazine *Challenges*, Angélus has seen "the land value of its vineyard double overnight, i.e., a virtual appreciation of over €200 million."[7]

And what about all these properties that gained the right to merge? Canon, a *premier grand cru classé B*, swallowed up Matras, which was simply a *grand cru classé*. The same thing for Trotte Vieille (*grand cru classé B*), which took over Bergat (simple *grand cru classé*). So many fabulous land deals and miraculous elevations of terroirs. "Trotte Vieille didn't have a second wine on the market,"[8] Philippe Castéja, owner of Trotte Vieille and a Bordeaux merchant, is said to have told the critic Jean-Marc Quarin. Second wines are less prestigious and less expensive wines that can't be part of the assemblage of the finest *grands crus*. The critic adds, with false naïveté, "Obviously, now there's nothing to prevent all the grapes from Bergat from going into the assemblage of Trotte Vieille!"[9] Yet another chance to increase profits!

Everyone is amused by the way customs have changed in this milieu: the grand principles of yesterday have quickly been swept aside. Although the 1986 classification had forcibly ejected Beau-Séjour Bécot for having dared to integrate Château La Carte into its land holdings, today the same château can swallow up another estate, La Gomerie, which isn't classified, and no one blinks an eye. "What a reversal of history! That was another time and a different economy!"[10] says Quarin ironically.

For many years, and still today, Saint-Émilion has prided itself on maintaining its classification of historic terroirs, while Médoc only classified brands. The right bank criticized the left bank for being motivated only by financial gain, with well-known properties growing considerably over time, absorbing more modest terroirs so there could be more bottles with the label *premier* or *second cru classé*.

People used to say that while the left bank was inclined to sell off its grand principles, the right bank would never go down that road. But the market must have been more powerful than the resolve of the people of Saint-Émilion.

"These economic realities will titillate the imagination of people who believe in beautiful stories where you pay dearly for unique eternal values where terroir and nature play the essential role,"[11] says Jean-Marc Quarin ironically.

While average terroirs were able to climb to the highest ranks in this new classification thanks to sales strategies or land opportunities, good terroirs were, on the contrary, downgraded. In particular, this was the case with Croque-Michotte. Yet from its terrace, surrounded by hundred-year-old trees, you can see Pétrus, the single greatest Pomerol, and Cheval Blanc, one of the *premiers grands crus classés A* of Saint-Émilion. La Dominique (Saint-Émilion *grand cru classé*) and the prestigious Pomerols Gazin and L'Évangile are also a stone's throw from Croque-Michotte. Despite these illustrious neighbors, the terroir of this château is apparently worthless.

"To hear the commission tell it, there's a geological black hole in the middle of this zone of the most illustrious vineyards and it's exactly where Croque-Michotte is located,"[12] remarks Pierre Carle, the self-assured Protestant manager of this château. His immediate neighbors, the Girauds, share in this bad luck, since their estate, La Tour du Pin Figeac, was also declassified. Their land is said to lack homogeneity. Curiously, the adjacent plot of land, which was sold by the Moueix family to Cheval Blanc in 2007, doesn't have any problems. In fact, 1.38 hectares were integrated into the land of the prestigious château of Bernard Arnault and Albert Frère. Strangely enough, Croque-Michotte and La Tour du Pin Figeac both regularly received substantial purchase offers from their prestigious neighbors. And both always refused. "It's certain that I have neighbors who own very big châteaux and would like to expand," Pierre Carle says wryly. And all of Saint-Émilion talks about the views that La Dominique has of Croque-Michotte and that Cheval Blanc has of La Tour du Pin Figeac. These rumors are energetically denied by Cheval Blanc.

"These guys have a plantation mentality; they want to buy up everything around them. And they'll stop at nothing to do it. They have the people who don't want to sell to them declassified. Then they go to see them a few months later, when they're struggling financially, to offer them a check. A small one, of course, because the vineyard is declassified, and because they don't have any choice: their land isn't worth anything anymore, nor is their wine, and they can't pay off their loans. These neofeudal lords wait a while, a more or less decent delay, and then make the declassified plots of land part of their land with the OK of the National Institute for Origin and Quality that doesn't notice a thing. And voilà, they've got a *premier grand cru classé* for a steal!,"[13] says a winemaker who knows the customs of the region.

Being declassified obviously means financial death. First of all because the winemakers have all taken out big loans to apply for classification. "The winemakers are forced to do massive renovations so their place looks like a Renaissance château. Refusing to play the game means they'll definitely be declassified,"[14] laments Dominique Techer. So they make the most gigantic investments they can. "No one talks about terroir and wine around here anymore. They just talk about all the trimmings that go with it," grumbles a winemaker who is nevertheless pleased to have gotten a great deal on barrel-shelving equipment from Troplong Mondot, a château that was hoping to become a *premier grand cru classé B*.[15] "I got this new equipment for a third of the price because the owners were afraid that the color of these shelves would clash with the rest of their cellar and that such bad taste would destroy their hopes of being classified." They all get deeply into debt and yet they won't all get or keep the precious classified status. For the declassified, it's doubly painful: the price of their wine and land collapses, and they still have to pay off the loans they've taken out to compete.

That's usually when the wolves come out of their lairs and suggest a friendly conversation.

19

PESTICIDE VICTIMS

She's a young woman with limitless determination. She speaks in a calm, soft voice. Except when she talks about pesticides. Then, her eyes become hard. She never loses her cool, but she takes on a fighting stance. Like a boxer, she tucks her head into her shoulders and hunches over.

This small woman is Marie-Lys Bibeyran. She works in the vineyards, like her father, a retired cellar master, and like her husband, who works for a prestigious château in Médoc. Her brother, Denis, also works in wine. The job is in the family's blood.

Marie-Lys's father passed this legacy on to all his offspring. But today he regrets it bitterly. His love of the vineyards has cost him a great deal. It took his son, who died of cancer suddenly at age forty-seven. Marie-Lys is sure her brother died from all the pesticides he had to handle. "He thought he was safe living in the country! He led a healthy life. He didn't smoke; he didn't drink. His only mistake was his job growing grapes." This hard work exposed him to dangerous chemicals on a daily basis. "His job was to apply pesticides. He mixed them up, filled the vats, sprayed, and then cleaned the equipment. And he did it for almost twenty-five years."[1]

When he found out he was going to die, he asked scientists about what might have caused the cancer. They said that it would take twenty years to find out for sure what caused it. The illness would catch up to him well before that.

This death sentence didn't keep him from fighting—on the contrary. Denis wanted to know what had poisoned him. Yet, all around him, there was a code of silence. His relatives and his winegrowing friends didn't like his determination. In this agricultural milieu, people are quiet, and they suffer in silence. Like a curse. "When you have cancer, you don't have a lot of friends left, and when on top of that you're a farm worker and you dare to ask bothersome questions, you don't have any left at all,"[2] says Marie-Lys, her voice faltering.

Cancer didn't leave Denis enough time to see his fight through to the end. On his deathbed, his sister swore to take up the fight for him, like a legacy she had to uphold. She doesn't want her brother's death to have been in vain. She wants farmers who get sick to be supported by legislation, which is currently inadequate. Most cancers caused by pesticides aren't recognized as occupational illnesses. While we wait for the laws to change, these substances have devastating effects in our countryside, and the farmers don't have the right to be recognized as victims of the pesticides they apply.

Marie-Lys has done everything she can to have her brother's cancer recognized as an occupational illness. She called the Agricultural Social Mutual Fund of Gironde, the farmers' health service. They were suspicious. "They said, 'Why are you doing this? How will it help you? You want money, right?' They thought I must be in it for the money . . . I had a terrible time getting the information and the explanations how to get the necessary documents. You have to really be determined or you'd just drop it."[3]

But Marie-Lys is tenacious. She dealt with all these obstacles and decided to ask her brother's employer to list the chemicals he was exposed to during the twenty-four years he worked for this estate. She met with the vineyard owner. The winemaker who employed her brother for years grudgingly provided her with a list of the products to which Denis was exposed for the last seven years he worked there. But he provided no more than that; the rest was lost. He became heated, giving veiled threats: "Think it over before you start this. Don't smear my reputation or you'll be sorry."[4] He also asked her if she was after money. She left the meeting devastated. As if almost a quarter century of shared hard work had been erased.

"We're not talking about a year or two of work, but twenty-four years, side by side. My brother thought of his employers almost like friends. Then all of a sudden, you feel it's all nothing. There's only monetary interest, the fear of losing money and their sacrosanct reputation."[5]

Such behavior only redoubled this intrepid woman's determination. But she hadn't predicted that since she seemed too tough to handle, these people would lash out at her brother's widow and her own father. "I thought I would be the target. I didn't even imagine they could go after my father. An old man who had just buried his son."[6]

They told her father that if his daughter persisted, he would have no friends left. They told her sister-in-law that Marie-Lys was crazy and wanted to dig up Denis's body. They were both shaken by this, but stood by Marie-Lys, who realized that she needed to go beyond her personal story and help other families who were grieving because of pesticides. She wanted to give them proof of the poisoning, a weapon to fight with. She came up with the idea of analyzing winegrowers' hair and the hair of residents near treated fields. She wanted to know how many pesticides are absorbed by people who simply live near these châteaux but are suffering the collateral damage.

To fund this research, she worked with Générations Futures, an antipesticide organization. Kudzu Science laboratories analyzed the hair of fifteen vineyard workers and five local residents. A control group of five people who lived far from the vineyards was also tested. "I focused on Listrac, in Médoc, where I live and work and where my brother worked," explains Marie-Lys. "Plus, in this town, there are all kinds of vineyards: a large cooperative, small vineyard owners, and also big châteaux. I didn't want only one or two well-known châteaux to be targeted [in particular, Clarke, an estate purchased in 1973 by Baron Edmond de Rothschild, is located in Listrac]. I tried to cover all the types of vineyards in the town, and all ages. I wanted it to be as representative as possible."[7]

Marie-Lys was ready for criticism. "Of course, it isn't a very big sample, but each analysis cost almost three hundred euros." A significant budget for a woman with limited income. "Nothing is stopping the health agencies from investigating this on a larger scale," Marie-Lys adds pointedly. For the results of this microstudy are incontrovertible. Even though the "guinea pigs" of the sample didn't directly handle pesticides, the lab found they had eleven times more residues than the control group who lived far from the vineyards (an average of 6.6 pesticides, versus .6). And there were five times more pesticide residues on the local residents than on the control group (an average of 3 pesticide residues versus .06).

The lab found ten different pesticides on the hair of four out of the fifteen winegrowers. This sorry record is held by the employees of the big Médoc châteaux. "I don't understand their strategy," Marie-Lys says sadly. "These people have an image to uphold. How can they take the risk of having a sick employee? It's as if a human life is less important to them than a grapevine." These big names were not happy about her investigation, especially when they were mentioned in the media. One of her friends who worked for a large estate was threatened with losing his job in barely veiled terms.

These results certainly do look bad for one of the most prestigious Bordeaux regions. The analysis revealed a banned chemical, diuron, on the hair of one of the workers.

Over 45 percent of the products that were identified by the lab are classified as possible carcinogens in Europe or the United States and 36 percent are suspected of being endocrine disruptors.

The workers themselves were the most surprised of all at these results. "At first, they participated without much conviction, mostly to make me happy. But when they saw their results, they realized it was true. They're risking their health on a daily basis when they go to work."[8]

Marie-Lys watches the rain hit the windowpanes of her apartment. The pesticide sellers are lobbying hard on the estates. They're omnipresent at the vineyards. With all the rain this year, they're playing Cassandra to the worried winemakers. "They say the estate is in danger. That the vines are covered with disease. That they absolutely have to use chemicals. And they've always got the miracle product that will save the harvest from all these ills."[9] She stops and glances through the window. "I call them merchants of death. They're like vultures over their prey."[10]

Marie-Hélène is a very pretty woman in her fifties. She's one of the local residents who agreed to have their hair analyzed. She's lived 150 meters from a vineyard for twenty-five years. "The grapevines came five years after me!" she clarifies. "I like to mention that because when I start complaining about pesticides, people always say, 'You didn't have to move here!' But in my case, I was here before the vineyard!"[11] She describes her daily existence. "Every summer, it's the same thing when we're eating outside. It's like they do it on purpose, the tractors come at one o'clock and they spray without worrying whether we're inside or not. So we quickly grab our trays and head indoors quick as we can!"[12] But these little inconveniences that are part of the usual tribulations of the neighborhood take on another dimension when this calm woman talks about the pains in her stomach. "In the beginning, you don't really pay attention. But over time, I start thinking, my God, all those chemicals . . . And all those plants dying in my garden."[13]

So she decided to participate in the investigation and to reveal her identity to the media. Not easy when you're the local *boulangère*. And, in fact, some people stopped buying bread from her overnight. But Marie-Hélène doesn't regret her actions. Now she knows. On her hair they found three pesticides, two endocrine disruptors and a carcinogen. Clearly, there are risks, even if it's still difficult to assess them.

Marie-Hélène is worried not just for herself, but also for her family. Her daughter just had a miscarriage. She wonders, as any mother would, if it also might be linked to pesticides. It seems uncertain in this specific case, but how can she be sure when the health authorities seem paralyzed by inertia or fear? Fear of what? Meanwhile, racked with guilt over having raised her children in a world that could turn out to be dangerous, Marie-Hélène broods.

In Listrac that day, it rains intermittently and there are gusts of wind. It's the day of the Fête de la Fleur. And while a fancy circus is being prepared at Château Lagrange and people await radiant stars who bring their aura and prestige to the wine industry, the vineyards are being sprayed with pesticides.

Ever since the decree of September 12, 2006, pesticides must not be sprayed when the wind is above nineteen kilometers per hour. That day, it reaches fifty-five kilometers per hour. Marie-Lys questions a man who is spraying products on the field. He gets off his tractor threateningly and explains that he's applying fertilizers, not pesticides.

She turns to me, mockingly: "I have big news for you. The winemakers in Listrac don't use pesticides at all anymore. It's that simple, they've all gone organic! For recently when I see them massively applying products, every single one told me it was fertilizer!"[14] She doesn't back down and looks him straight in the eye. In a rage, he gets back on his tractor.

"They must really think we're idiots,"[15] says this warrior of the vineyards.

For how much longer?

20

THE ONE WHO SAID NO

He has a severe Protestant manner and the slightly out-of-date appearance of all these down-on-their-luck grand families who don't have the funds to match their legacy anymore. And while Château Croque-Michotte has maintained its bourgeois elegance, the warped parquet and the water marks betray a cruel lack of money. This beautiful building with its old-fashioned charm is indeed a far cry from the palaces that have been renovated with millions of euros by all the nouveaux riches who have invaded Bordeaux wine country. But its manager, Pierre Carle—the great-grandson of Samuel Geoffrion, who purchased it in 1906—is determined to keep up the family estate.

But it seems the sharks of the enchanted kingdom have another plan. Pierre Carle has had a hard time making his business work ever since his château was, as most people agree, unfairly declassified. He could've left it at that. Felt sorry for himself. Or, even better, sworn allegiance to the local barons. Many others before him followed that path. But it's not his habit to bow and scrape. He's an iron-willed man who intends to resist. With him, the sharks hit a snag.

It all started in 2006—a date that sounded the alarm bell for the respectability of the Saint-Émilion classification. Not that this ritual hadn't ever been challenged in the past: it happened with every new version. But before this fateful date, everything was usually settled "between friends." Until then, "they" (meaning the wine syndicate) came to an arrangement and "they" gently let the declassified vineyards know that it was not in their interest to fight this too hard. But in 2006, they found themselves facing this incorruptible Protestant who refused to give in. A man over whom the local microcosm never had any control because he isn't from Saint-Émilion and doesn't aspire to be part of its cliques. "He doesn't give off the right pheromones to be part of the milieu, but, unlike all the others, he just doesn't care,"[1] laughs Dominique Techer, the old-style, slightly anarchist winemaker located on the prestigious Pomerol plateau.

Pierre Carle has no use for all these newcomers, these rich capitalists who settled in Saint-Émilion to make money. He defends this Bordeaux land with his heart and soul, even though he was never welcomed here. "In Saint-Émilion, you have to either be an aristocrat or want to make money. He doesn't fit into either of these categories,"[2] smiles Dominique Techer. Pierre Carle admits this easily: "We have a vineyard near Bergerac [an unprestigious wine-growing area not far from Saint-Émilion], and we can see the difference in the mentality. Here, there's no way to get on to the Saint-Émilion Council. It's all locked up by a few people who control everything."[3]

So in 2006 this defiant man decided to go to war against the declassification of Croque-Michotte.[4] And he won. That shows how tenacious he is. Saint-Émilion couldn't get over seeing its wonderful classification declared invalid due to absurd criteria. The wine world took it very badly. And the châteaux that were promoted in the controversial and chaotic 2006 classification, the places that had all spent lots of money to obtain this precious status, were not at all happy that their classification didn't stand. So the case would go on to have many unexpected and unusual legal developments.

Act I: The INAO, paying little attention to the criteria that it was supposed to have verified, published the classification, which was immediately approved by interministerial decree and signed by the agriculture minister at the time, Dominique Bussereau, on December 12, 2006.

Act II: A Bordeaux court struck down the classification on July 1, 2008, ruling against the minister and INAO. This decision, which passed unnoticed in the media at the time, was like a thunderclap in the republic of Saint-Émilion, where such matters are not usually decided in the light of day.

If the classification is overturned, then those who were promoted are no longer promoted. In a rage, the eight vineyards that lost their promotions[5] decided to put on the third act of this tragicomedy and filed lawsuit after lawsuit, losing them all.[6] The judges were not moved by the suffering of all these big Bordeaux names! They then appealed to the Council of State, the supreme administrative court.

Oddly enough, the Saint-Émilion Wine Council, the wine syndicate that is supposed to represent all the winemakers in the appellation, became a party to the suit. "So this means that these people, whose duty is to represent all of us without distinction, decided to go to court with a few winemakers, against other winemakers, at the expense of all the winemakers,"[7] observes Pierre Carle ironically. To say this is surprising is putting it mildly. The final twist: on November 29, 2011, shortly before the Council of State was to hear the case, the Saint-Émilion Wine Council and six of the plaintiffs threw in the towel and dropped the case. Two vineyards[8] stubbornly persisted and were definitively rejected by the Council of State on Friday, December 23, 2011. A historic date for the enchanted kingdom.

The legal wrangling was over, but Act IV turned political. The classification means money, and losing it means taking a huge financial hit. So it was unthinkable not to restore some semblance of hierarchy by giving a second chance to those who lost classification and integrating those who had gained it. The Saint-Émilion Wine Council has a lot of influence. It sought the support of two Gironde department politicians, Senator Gérard César and Representative Jean-Paul Garraud (who was defeated in the legislative elections of 2012). Two officials who put in a lot of effort because they managed to save if not Saint-Émilion's honor at least the framework of the classification thanks to two riders that were stealthily inserted into bills up for voting. And this is the happy ending of the farce. Thanks to the first rider slipped into article 106 of the law on modernization of the economy[9] of August 4, 2008, those who lost classification in 2006 were allowed to keep it until 2009.

Alas, those who were promoted and then rejected lost out. So the officials entered the fray once again to insert another amendment, this one slipped into the law[10] of May 12, 2009. Thus the eight vineyards that were promoted and then demoted got the right to maintain their classification until 2011, even though this classification no longer existed because it had been nullified by the courts. An incredible privilege.

The cautious wine council, which wasn't totally sure of the outcome of its numerous maneuvers, had gone ahead and discreetly launched a new classification with the INAO. A new classification for which the châteaux who were applying had already paid some €618,000 to have the privilege of participating in.[11] This €618,000 had already been partly spent in procedures and counterprocedures to create the classification standards for 2012. The INAO would have had to pay back this €618,000 if the wine council had prevailed at the Council of State to reestablish the 2006 classification. No matter, the taxpayers would have paid for all these whims.

So obviously the mood was heavy in Saint-Émilion in the months preceding the publication of the 2012 classification. The town kept up appearances, boasting that the INAO's classification was a guarantee of the quality of its wine. But behind the scenes a war was raging. Everyone wanted to be rewarded in accordance with their hopes.

Those who were declassified in 2006 wanted to be reclassi-fied. Those who were promoted wanted to keep their pro-motion, not counting all those who had been disappointed and were determined not to let this chance get away from them again.

Although Pierre Carle managed to have the 2006 clas-sification struck down, he wasn't able to impress the INAO commission in the 2012 version. What an unfortunate coin-cidence; he was declassified once more! Convinced that he wouldn't dare rise up against them again, the local potentates had no scruples about excluding him. They had to punish this obstinate rebel. Even better, they put pressure on him so that he wouldn't be likely to retaliate. "We were warned: 'Whoever challenges the classification will be exiled, ostra-cized,'" remembers the owner of a world-class *premier grand cru classé*. None of these tricks persuaded Pierre Carle to back down. Quite the opposite. He studied the new clas-sification and dissected it until he uncovered a system that was totally crazy. Along with two other declassified vine-yards, the Giraud family (Le Tour du Pin Figeac) and the Boidron family (Château Corbin Michotte), he decided to launch a dual attack against the classification. First they filed a lawsuit in administrative court. But this time, he also filed suit against X (in France, it is possible to sue someone who remains publicly anonymous, known only as X) for abuse of office. This X was Hubert de Boüard, who realized this and adopted the posture of a victim—something new for him—vehemently denouncing the treachery of this dreadful suit against him, the man of the common good who was thinking only of the appellation's future.

Since they couldn't make it look as if they were out to get one man, the plaintiffs also targeted Philippe Castéja,[12] a merchant who, like Hubert de Boüard, is a member of INAO's National Committee. Like his buddy, Castéja also gained from the classification by absorbing the terroir of one of his less prestigious properties into the land of his *premier grand cru classé*.

In their suit, the plaintiffs emphasized the two men's presence at certain crucial INAO meetings[13] about the classification. They had a court bailiff certify that the minutes of these meetings had conveniently disappeared from the site where they were previously located—before appearing there again. This game of hide-and-seek looked bad.

Despite the pressure, the fear of gossip, and the disapproval of the whole appellation that united behind Hubert de Boüard, Pierre Carle along with his lawsuit companions and their lawyer, François de Contencin, were determined to confront them. "My clients are very brave; I see them as the Three Musketeers,"[14] François de Contencin says. They certainly have the Musketeers' courage, along with a pinch of Don Quixote's madness.

They were determined not to give up, and when the court made the strange decision not to hear their case, they brought it before the senior investigating judge. At the same time, the other side also prepared for war and stockpiled weapons. In the minutes of the Saint-Émilion Wine Council board of directors meeting from May 21, 2013, we read that "considering the collective interest that the classification represents for all the wines of Saint-Émilion, the board of directors confirmed the necessity of defending it."

The Saint-Émilion Wine Council budgeted a trifling €60,000 for this defense. "The sum indicated in the budget was €45,000, which corresponds to the fees for the lawyers who are defending the classification. It seems that the plaintiffs are marshaling numerous resources that require thorough analysis. Therefore, we ask the board of directors to approve a budget of an additional €15,000 in order to develop the defense alongside the ministry."[15]

Faced with the possible prospect of the classification being rejected after this fierce battle, some winemakers became more understanding of the declassified ones, even suggesting they should be immediately classified if they dropped their lawsuit. This idea was coolly received by the president of the syndicate, Jean-François Quenin, who virtuously retorted that "the Wine Council has no power in this external procedure that is entirely handled by the Ministry of Agriculture and the INAO." Basically, the syndicate never had anything to do with this classification and never ever will. Of course, that's why the syndicate[16] allotted €45,000 for defending it and why the local elite gathered "to defend the classification, alongside the ministry."[17]

People with a mischievous sense of humor will find a little sentence in these minutes that may make them laugh. Once again, it's about the sponsor of this wonderful classification. "Concerning the presidencies of the divisions, the president reports that Hubert de Boüard wishes to step back a bit and withdraw as president of the Saint-Émilion division and the Saint-Émilion Grand Cru division."[18] The great man would like to distance himself a bit from his syndicate to quiet the gossips and the rebel elements. Better late than never. In other words, this little world stands together to support the precious classification, whatever the cost.

The lawyer for the declassified vineyards sticks to his guns: "This case will change things. This classification is a real scandal; it's not acceptable that the winners are part of the national bodies of INAO! This case isn't striking out at certain individuals, but at the way a public organization operates."[19]

Indeed, the entire way the profession is organized—and the murky role of the INAO—is on trial.

21

A LITTLE GUY
AMONG THE GREATS

This story calls to mind the fable of an envious little frog that wanted to be as big as an ox. He constantly "swells and inflates himself and struggles to become as big as this animal"—to the point where he explodes.

> *This world of ours is full of foolish creatures too—*
> *Commoners want to build châteaux;*
> *Each princeling wants his royal retinue;*
> *Each counts his squires. And so it goes.*[1]

Jean de La Fontaine could have added: each *second cru* wants to be *premier*.

While the unavoidable Hubert de Boüard de Laforest is perceived by the nobodies as a big shot, it's amusing to observe that for the historic *premiers grands crus*, he will never be anything but an ugly duckling, a peasant who wouldn't stay in his place, an upstart who should be punished for daring to rise so high in the hierarchy of the kingdom.

Hubert is quite aware of this and quietly inveighs against the estates that have been at the pinnacle for many years and want nothing to do with him or "the grocer" Gérard Perse, the owner of Pavie who made his fortune in supermarkets and gradually climbed the rungs of the social ladder. "The wine world is just like any other closed society. When five or six guests are seated around a fine meal, people generally don't like seeing a seventh guest arrive,"[2] says the distressed Hubert, now suddenly very small in the midst of these lords.

So, disinclined to share, are these historic *premiers grands crus* displeased to see these two newcomers arrive? But although Gérard Perse attracts even more scorn than Hubert (imagine, an ex–house painter who isn't even from Bordeaux), all the hatred is focused on his flamboyant buddy. Hubert the overactive. Hubert who is always everywhere. Hubert who was able to develop his network when the elite didn't see him coming.

He's kind of like the Nicolas Sarkozy of the vineyards: disliked but omnipresent and efficient, at least when defending his interests—and why not?—and promoting his friends.

The system is under enormous pressure, or perhaps even about to implode.

Therefore, when Pierre Carle wanted to attack the classification, he found a sympathetic ear at one of the historic *grands crus* on the Saint-Émilion hill. This tough, extremely upstanding man—who must remain anonymous and had

to fight hard to keep his wine in the family and raise it to
the level where it is today—listened to Carle and decided
to break the law of silence, at the risk of turning the newly
promoted vineyards against him. Given this man's position,
all of his opinions are closely scrutinized. He can't risk speaking openly. If he did, the whole structure would crumble,
and, with it, many small winemakers who rely on the classification to make their reputation. So he takes action, but in
the shadows. He helps the declassified vineyards, constantly
digging through the regulations and uncovering new pro-
cedural flaws day after day.

It pained him to see Angélus and Pavie rise to wine-
making heights that he doesn't think they deserve, and he
even suggested a solution to the INAO: create a higher
level, kind of like an A+, for Ausone and Cheval Blanc. The
INAO, very close to Hubert de Boüard and aware of the
ridiculousness of the situation, naturally refused any change.
It was impossible, without acknowledging the inanity of
the classification, to create another paradise where the two
newcomers would not be allowed.

Since the INAO would not let this historic member of
the A group inflict the affront that he believed his adversary
deserved, he put all his energy into preventing him from
being accepted by the other *premiers grands crus classés*. "He
may have the classification, but he certainly doesn't have the
status," the anonymous *grand cru* winemaker asserts.

The most recent humiliation Hubert had to suffer was
not being accepted in the very select G9, a group of the top
five in Médoc: Château Lafite Rothschild, Château Latour,

Château Margaux, Château Mouton Rothschild, Château Haut-Brion, as well as the three icons from the right bank: Pétrus, Ausone, and Cheval Blanc, plus Château d'Yquem, the most recent member.

"The G9 has been around forever, it's an informal group, for sharing everything regarding their wine, status, techniques, and biodynamics. They set their own standards. This club works very well and one thing is clear: they don't want Angélus or Pavie!" says a knowledgeable observer of the Bordeaux wine world.

This sticks in Hubert's craw. He tells anyone who will listen that Frédéric Engerer, head of Latour, offered to make him part of the G9, but all the others were dead set against it and voted it down. "I have no memory of this vote or this meeting," said one of the *premiers grands crus classés* of Saint-Émilion, suddenly struck by amnesia.

When you ask why the lords left these two applicants at the door, the answer is crystal clear and definitive: "To put it frankly, the two newcomers don't have the same problems or the same standards as we do."

Most of all, it's Hubert the Conqueror's manners that offend them. "This guy works a lot, especially for himself, but . . . a little bit for the others, too, I have to admit," adds one of the historical kings archly. "The problem is his bad manners. As soon as he's classified, right away he makes demands, he calls, he stamps his foot impatiently. He wants everything, right away. This nouveau riche thing—'I have arrived'—is absolutely unbearable."

If he wants to continue to rise to the heavens, Hubert will have to be more patient with his illustrious colleagues. He still lacks the necessary composure to put up with the little humiliations to which his rank of newcomer inevitably exposes him.

During a tasting, Cheval Blanc's young, elegant technical director, Pierre-Olivier Clouet, perhaps a little gauchely, or simply to tease, emphasized that Angélus was at the bottom of the hill (meaning on terroirs that were less noble). Deeply hurt, Hubert had picked up the phone and yelled at Pierre Lurton, the boss of this young screwup. The elegant director of Cheval Blanc remembers with amusement this little scene, which he didn't appreciate. "I was holding the phone over fifty centimeters away so my eardrum wouldn't explode. He yelled about my employees and ordered me to keep them in line. I calmed him down. It was out of the question to add fuel to the fire. But I really wanted to say, 'Hubert, whether you like it or not, you *are* at the bottom of the hill!'"[3]

In fact, the market hasn't recognized either Angélus or Pavie as being part of Saint-Émilion royalty. "They don't have the same status as we do," one of the historic barons put it bluntly. "In 2012, Ausone 2011 was priced three or four times more than Angélus. And there's even more of a difference with Pavie. And when Mouton Rothschild was promoted, it had been more expensive than Lafite for forty years," argues this *premier grand cru classé*.

This comparison is interesting when you know how hard Baron Philippe de Rothschild, Mouton's charismatic owner, had to fight to have his wine move up from *second* to *premier*. It was his lifelong struggle. Wasn't the motto of this famous château a nod to that of the Rohan family:[4] *"Premier ne puis, second ne daigne, Mouton suis.* [First, I cannot be, second, I deign not to be, Mouton am I.]" However, the baron held all the cards: he was from a grand family with impressive connections and he also instituted a number of innovations in the wine industry. Starting in 1924, he had his wine bottled at the château; until then the wine had been delivered in barrels to the merchants. The idea was naturally to get more control over his wine and to counterbalance the merchants' great power. So he had to increase storage capacities at the château, but instead of doing it in a small way, and with a grasp of the importance of public relations much earlier than his peers, he had his cellar built by the architect Charles Siclis.

And what better way to make a name for yourself than to bring on board talented contemporary artists to create a legendary label for Mouton every year? Starting in 1924, he called on the poster artist Jean Carlu. But not until Philippe Julian's famous V for victory in 1945 did this "call to artists" become Mouton's trademark. Since then, the wine has had labels by the greatest names: from Jean Cocteau to Braque, from César to Miró, from Chagall to Kandinsky, from Warhol to Soulages, from Niki de Saint-Phalle to Francis Bacon—and even Prince Charles of England! All these big names create buzz every year.

However, despite his talent and power—he became a giant of the Bordeaux wine trade—Rothschild had to wait until 1973 and the good graces of a minister of agriculture who would later become president, Jacques Chirac, before the supposedly unchangeable classification of Médoc would finally open up for him. Half a century of networking to finally attain paradise! And change his motto: "First I am, second I was, Mouton changes not."

And yet this promotion was not all smooth sailing, for it displeased many: Count Alexandre de Lur Saluces, who was then the owner of the iconic Château d'Yquem, appealed in vain this decree signed by Chirac. Fighting already!

Some forty years later, Mouton is still, in the eyes of the local lords, an upstart that doesn't totally belong at the table. "A few years ago, Prince Robert de Luxembourg, the head of Haut-Brion, one of the historic *premiers crus*, organized a vertical tasting [where several vintages of the same wine are tasted] of the *premiers grands crus* of Médoc with the Grand Jury European. Fabulous vintages of these marvelous wines were served," Jean-Luc Thunevin remembers fondly. "And when I was surprised that Mouton wasn't served at this fantastic tasting, I received the scathing answer, 'Well, Mouton wasn't classified in 1855!'" he recalls, laughing. "In other words, if Angélus and Pavie have the classification . . . they aren't close to having their A status!"[5]

They will have to be patient and wait a few more years before they can hope for any recognition from their illustrious colleagues. Pierre Lurton, head of Cheval Blanc, is categorical: for *premiers grands crus classés*, the first two hundred years are the hardest.

22

TRIBULATIONS OF A BORDEAUX WINEMAKER IN CHINA

"He's the fifth-richest man in China; you have to see him," implores this young Bordeaux merchant during a magical evening hosted by one of the countless barons in the region— Hubert de Boüard, him again—during the *en primeur* sales. His cellar with the famous upside-down conical vats has been transformed into a magnificent disco for the occasion. The effect is stunning. The lights are reflected on the sides of the gigantic vats hanging from the ceiling.

The self-satisfied Bordeaux jet set has hurried to this baroque location to be as close as possible to the new holder of the top classification level. Everyone pats him on the back. They want to touch, approach, congratulate, and thank him. "If some day I don't make wine anymore, I'll turn this into a nightclub," he boasts.

All of the guests, including those from China, are charmed. The young merchant launches another salvo. "I'll bring them to meet you at Angélus tomorrow; it would be great to give them the whole shebang." Meaning: a VIP tasting followed by a tour of the site. The owner is clearly not thrilled with the idea but he agrees. He gives these precious clients a salesman's smile and walks off.

The next day, he would be there as promised to welcome them in style. "You have to deal with it. I'm not excited about seeing them, but that's where the buying power is now,"[1] he admits. So he has to play the game. And work long days. Plus, Hubert is a marvelous storyteller. He receives them in his other château, Bellevue. He uses the occasion to rewrite his family history and explain that he was born a stone's throw away from this fabulous property. He describes in great detail his battle to take back this château, which had fallen into other hands at an earlier time. To hear him tell it, his life is an eternal battle from which he always emerges victorious. The buyers are enthralled. Hubert certainly has an aura.

Then he takes them to Angélus, which is under construction. They stop by the bells and, with a magical touch of the remote control, the Chinese national anthem begins to play. The lord of the manor flashes an ultrabright smile. The guests are moved. And they warmly thank their host before going to have a private tasting of Angélus.

They have brought him a present: a triptych of traditional Chinese lacquer paintings. Hubert looks at the gift disdainfully and later forgets it on the mantel. The young merchant, who speaks fluent Mandarin, handles the translation. Joyfully, she tells Hubert that these clients with incredible buying power would like him to become their consultant for a project they want to start up in China. All the necessary resources will be at his disposal to create the best vineyard in China.

The young merchant is bubbling with excitement. But Hubert de Boüard seems impassive. "That's very nice of them, but for now I have no free time,"[2] he says. Clearly unaccustomed to getting the cold shoulder, these powerful clients sweeten the deal. He can name his price; they're ready to invest millions. "Yes, yes, very nice. I'll be free for Vinexpo 2014 but not before. We'll see about it then,"[3] he says, brushing them off. The merchant rushes around like a madwoman, announces that she's ready to leave immediately to oversee construction and examine the vineyards on site. "Great idea," he smiles. "Go ahead. Young people should see the world."[4] Upon my surprise at his lack of enthusiasm, he explains, "With this kind of clientele, it's always the same thing: they want to create something fantastic right away, right now. If you show you're interested, they scorn you. They use you and throw you away like an old Kleenex. You have to keep them at arm's length; it's the only thing they understand. They want the Angélus brand. That's what they want to buy. Well, you have to earn this brand; you have to desire it,"[5] he declares with satisfaction. Then he adds mockingly, "I can tell you from experience that it's in my interest to wait a year. I've seen lots of fifth-richest men in China come through here who, the following year, were bankrupt, in liquidation, or, even worse, in prison. No one should be fooled; they're often bandits."[6]

Despite its harshness and cynicism, the Chinese gold mine attracts many. Rothschild, the proprietor of Lafite, set up shop in Shandong; LVMH, the owner of the legendary Cheval Blanc, in a city named Shangri-La at the foothills of Tibet. The billion-strong population and the double-digit growth of this country are enough to stimulate the craziest of appetites.

Michel Rolland has also headed for the land of the Forbidden City. Cofco, a food industry leader and the biggest wine producer in China, snapped up the most famous oenologist in Pomerol to handle its wine, Great Wall, with 140 million bottles produced each year. Of course, Michel Rolland doesn't oversee the entire line but vouches for the high-end part of it. The labels bear his signature, which is worth gold. And Rolland goes there only twice a year[7] to spread the good word to these faraway lands.

Stéphane Derenoncourt also went to conquer this new frontier. Courted by a big company specializing in real estate and energy, he is also supposed to create the best wine in China. A sweet utopia that already took the Rothschilds, LVMH, Rolland, and many others there before him. In fact, they all go there especially for the fabulous fees that this modern El Dorado represents: an average of €150,000 per year. You just can't turn down such sums, whatever reluctance these gentlemen may have to enter this foreign world.

It is often hard for them to understand each other: most Chinese speak English badly (in any case, no better than the French do), and the French don't know Mandarin.

Often, the Bordeaux winemakers do business through an intermediary. Djing, a young woman around forty who is married to a French engineer, works with the energetic Stéphane Derenoncourt. She's a very ambitious businesswoman who primarily works in finance but realized that there was business to be done by helping the French to get set up in China, since they clearly don't understand anything about the Chinese mentality. "When I saw your compatriots waste a crazy amount of energy and big sums of money in China just to end up with nothing, I realized there was a market,"[8] she says with a smile.

She got in touch with Stéphane Derenoncourt through Patrick Baseden, an upper-middle-class gentleman who first worked for Veuve Clicquot. Djing looks at Baseden with scorn. The French winemakers are there for only one reason, to help her reach her goal as quickly as possible, whatever the cost: to create the best Chinese wine in two years. In this quest for the holy grail, the company that hired her is willing to spend whatever it takes. It has allocated €25 million. But when you put so much money on the table, you tend to want to defy the laws of nature. What, a grapevine takes five years to grow? What, only one harvest per year? What, you can't create the best wine in the world in six months? If Djing could hang plastic grapes for the visitors and import wine from Latin America, she would do it. In fact, that's precisely what lots of people do: buy a château in Bordeaux and, once they have the label, sell fraudulent wine.

Stéphane Derenoncourt went to China with two members of his team: David Picci, a charismatic Italian nicknamed Il Dottore who is a veritable magician of the grapevines, and Romain Bocchio, a fiery thirty-something who dreams of adventure. With his two sidekicks and his old Bordeaux friend, Derenoncourt goes to his new employer's headquarters to taste local wines with the company's second-in-command. It's a clever way to show his partners that you can easily do better when you know how to invest. The three associates laugh until they cry over how wretched the wines are and what outrageous prices they sell for. In China, price all but determines quality. So selling mediocre wines at high prices is tantamount to making fine wine. Only the local trendsetting elite—they exist—which is more snobby and educated, refuses this way of thinking, preferring to buy foreign wines to be sure of their quality. French wine and New Zealand milk are their daily fare. A significant number of these bad Chinese wines already have Bordeaux oenologists as consultants.

Derenoncourt was approached to consult for two vineyards for the group. Both are located in the Xinjiang region. The first one is in Manasi, two and a half hours by car from Ürümqi. It's on the plains, and the farmers who work on these 40 hectares of land belong to a cooperative. First there's a big meeting. The beautiful Djing translates feverishly what Romain, Stéphane's young employee, tells her. She feels very committed and is glad to learn more about wine making and pruning techniques. David, Il Dottore, strolls through the vineyard and shows grape-growing techniques patiently, step by step, to the farmers. Today, he's covering pruning, and there's a long way to go. The farmers were trained to produce large quantities of grapes (120 hectoliters per hectare, whereas *grands crus* generate 35) and now they must learn to produce quality. Not easy. Il Dottore is distraught over their lack of love for the finishing touches. The devil is always in the details.

Given the modest terroir, David Picci thinks they should make white wine. They'll make red. "It's on the plains and it's silty; they'll never make terroir wine on this land," says Stéphane Derenoncourt. "They can just hope it's not as bad as the others, and that's not very complicated."

The next day, he leaves for Tulufan, a three-and-a-half-hour drive. The team gets out on an arid, windblown steppe. This Uyghur region is majority Muslim and more or less independent from Beijing. It's another world that must be traversed in hours-long rides in kitschy minibuses chartered for tourists.

During these long hours on the road, Djing talks about China and explains how you must always go through the central government, even to buy a small piece of land. "We have to play the game. In the Uyghur region, there are three levels of power. The local authorities, the central government, and the former army that turned into a pseudogroup for citizen discussion. The three levels hate each other and are jealous of each other, and I have to juggle them, without offending them, without committing any faux pas. It's hours and hours of negotiations, dinners, lunches, just to get a little piece of land."[9] Wei Xu, the elegant businessman from Shanghai, also emphasized this essential feature: "In China, you have to 'fuss and bother' over people, or manage your relationships if you prefer. Everything is granted through special favors, a doctor's appointment, your children's school, land for producing wine. You absolutely have to pay attention to the officials and make enough 'fuss and bother.'" Wei learned this the hard way. One of the little films that he made to sell his wine on Chinese television was rejected by the government. It featured bottles of Châteauneuf-du-Pape. "Too religious," the government apparently said, immediately banning promoting the wine or showing the film. "'We don't talk about the pope in China!' I hadn't paid enough attention to the 'fuss and bother,'"[10] Wei admits, being a good sport about it.

It's out of the question for Djing to make the same mistake. So when the bus suddenly stops because sedans are parked across the road, blocking its way like in a bad Mafia movie, Djing knows exactly what's going on. Under cover of a polite welcome, the intimidation of the officials who came to meet her is clear. She urges the team to get out of the bus and go meet them. Facing Stéphane Derenoncourt and his colleagues are the head of the cooperative, the mayor of Turpan, and a few other local authorities. Djing was supposed to meet them directly on the land, a few kilometers farther, but they preferred to see her on the way. "To show us that they know what's going on and to put pressure on us: there's no chance of us missing each other, we got this land because the second-in-command at our multinational company is close friends with the governor and the company has big energy interests here. But the land should've gone to the cooperative."[11]

In other words, this is a welcome that sounds like a warning.

Now accompanied by his escort of officials, Stéphane Derenoncourt finds himself facing an arid, windblown land. The grapevines are in an appalling state. They're only hanging on because they're heavily irrigated and loaded with fertilizers. The mediocre wines are "corrected" with large amounts of tartaric or sulfuric acid. It's hydroponic viticulture where the grapevines are blasted with products, and the wines are, too. The self-assured Derenoncourt refuses to make wine there.

During the whole ride back, Djing is thoughtful. She's thinking of the company's CEO and probably fearing his reaction: the company has big interests in the Uyghur region. She hopes she hasn't endangered them with the refusal of this cursed plot of land.

23

THE CAP JACKPOT

The European Union's Common Agricultural Policy (CAP) provides agricultural subsidies to European farmers and has been greatly criticized for the high cost and negative environmental impact of its projects in France. Since the CAP is supposed to help farmers survive, you wouldn't think the wine lords of Bordeaux would be able to get their hands on this public money. Think again!

In fact, a close study of the beneficiaries of this public largesse is very instructive. We learn in particular that Grands Chais de France (Great Cellars of France), one of the giants of the French wine trade with revenue of €841 million in 2012, received €1.35 million in subsidies between 2011 and 2012. Castel Frères—the leading French wine company and owner of the wine store chain Nicolas, which is on five continents and handles some 640 million bottles of wine every year—received subsidies of €1.62 million between 2011 and 2012.

And what about the Bordeaux lobbying organizations? The Interprofessional Council of Bordeaux Wines, for example, which, in general opinion, didn't take a vow of poverty? It received the nice little sum of €6.08 million between 2011 and 2012.

And the famous circles that organize the *en primeur* sales every year and manage to lure the top critics from around the world into their web? They also get money from French taxes—€1.09 million for the Union of Grands Crus, one of Robert Parker's stops. And how much money for our devoted Alain Raynaud and his Right Bank Circle: €368,000 in 2011 to 2012! That's a generous payment for a very private circle of handpicked prosperous members.

And the new *premiers grands crus classés A*? Gérard Perse of Pavie and Hubert de Boüard? Perse, the wealthy self-made man, raked in €211,000 for Château Pavie, along with €73,200 in the name of another wine-making company. Let's recall that this man of the year of the *Revue du Vin de France* owns several properties including the very prestigious Pavie (a bottle costs about €300), shares in Château Monbousquet, and also L'Hostellerie de Plaisance, Relais, and Châteaux, whose kitchen was, until recently, run by the great chef Philippe Etchebest.

As for Hubert de Boüard, Château La Fleur Saint Georges received almost a million euros (€969,744.54) between 2010 and 2011, where he built his famous upside-down conical vats, which cost him the trifling sum of €900,000.[1] His investment was quickly profitable thanks to the EU's generosity! The owner admits this, in fact, and is pleased with himself for "using European funds as others have,"[2] adding, as a warning to his peers, "I won't name names, but there are a lot of them."[3] And he concludes in a slightly elitist vein that "if they only gave these subsidies to those who aren't able to grow, it would be a problem. What are you going to do with people who don't have the means?"[4]

So let's be glad that public money is going to the elite instead of to the needy, who surely wouldn't be able to use it wisely!

But Hubert is right when he says that he's not the only one who has benefited from this largesse: Brussels gave €297 million to French winemakers between 2009 and 2011 so that they could afford to buy vats worthy of James Bond. This money was given to our rich winemakers so they could redo their cellars, but also to promote Bordeaux wine and support its market. As if it needed support!

We can see why our Chinese friends, who are trying to do whatever it takes to launch their own vineyards, are so strongly opposed to aid to French winemakers. Remember: it only took a threat from Brussels to tax Chinese solar panels for the Chinese to promise to launch an investigation into the dumping of French wines.

That crisis is over, until the next one comes. But is China, this great buyer of French wines, really so wrong in its analysis?

24

Fear, or the Reign of Modern Oenology

"The wine world no longer relies on observation or amateurism. We're professionals. We codify each wine, we measure out all the products, we can describe everything. So we have a surgical precision in every technical action. We're not in dreamland. That time is in the past. We're facing fierce international competition. We have to fight in the global markets. In each wine we sell, there must be a marker, a style that has to come back every year. That's what the buyer wants. We can't sell wines that are totally different from one year to the next. Oenology, technical developments, and analyses of contaminants have made us more and more performative to satisfy the consumer. The wine world is now part of the food industry, and it functions with the same rules. When you buy a yogurt, you don't want to find a fly in it, right? It has to be perfect, every time. That's what the wine world is today."

This strong-willed man, whose southwestern accent softens his almost warlike tone, is Jean-Philippe Fort,[1] one of the consulting oenologists for Michel Rolland's laboratory. But while his illustrious boss is much more pragmatic and much less convinced of the genius of science (he prefers human genius), Jean-Philippe Fort is a firm believer in all the technological marvels that according to him have transformed the wine world and finally moved it into the long-awaited era of industry.

He walks through his lab, effortlessly describing the fabulous machines all around. His favorite? A kind of grater that extracts color and allows you to guess through many analyses what wine will become in the vat. Just by crushing a few grape seeds and skins, the expert can predict whether he's dealing with a future *grand cru* or a cheap wine. It's as reliable as a wine horoscope, and expensive, too.

In a year like 2013, when the grapes began to rot faster than the harvesters could pick them, the labs were filled. The winemakers rushed over, feverishly bringing their bags of sad-looking grapes up to the counter.

"Afterward, it's up to each individual winemaker," explains Jean-Philippe Fort. "We don't force them. Just like you can't force someone to go get a checkup or a blood test. If the winemaker would rather do things unconventionally and hide his head in the sand, that's his choice. But that's not very reliable."[2]

There's a little bit of finger-pointing, but this scientific language has seemed convincing. And, with worry in their eyes, the winemakers came to look for salvation in these old machines recycled from the medical industry, hoping that the oenologist, like a wine-making messiah, would produce a miracle to avert disaster.

"It's easy to impress those who don't know any better, and there's a lot of money in it,"[3] says wine consultant Stéphane Derenoncourt, who has made it his trademark to do without the whole arsenal of products as much as possible.

In 2013, like other years before it, there's no miracle in sight. The analyses were just there to confirm what they knew already from tasting their grapes: not yet ripe and most of them rotten already. But like patients with a terminal disease who keep going back for more tests, hoping against all hope that finally the doctors will find a last-minute cure, the winemakers came to soothe their immense worry in the labs.

"This year, the winemakers will go bust, but the fear-mongers will make a shitload of money," exclaims Dominique Techer, the Pomerol farmer. "When the winemakers do badly, their little chemistry business does great!"[4]

"It's definitely where the money's at," says an irritated Stéphane Derenoncourt. "Either you're a technical oenologist or you're a chef. I much prefer being a chef."[5]

He tells the amusing story of a day in 2007 right before the harvest when one of his new clients called in a total panic. "'Mr. Derenoncourt, I'm very worried. I'm looking at the cellar and it's empty.'

"'Yes, but tomorrow there will be grapes.'

"'But I mean there are no products! You're not going to tell me you make wine just with grapes?'

"He later apologized. He almost didn't hire us because we were too expensive, except that we aren't making huge margins on a whole line of reassuring gimmicks. I like the idea of making wine with grapes,"[6] he adds wryly.

And Derenoncourt observed that in hard years like 2013, to make good wine you had to be "creative." "The winemakers should know that there's nothing magic in all this chemical shit. It's just makeup, it won't last in the long run."[7] Dominique Techer is convinced of it, even if he acknowledges that in the worst years these products were a crutch for those who would have lost everything otherwise. But he doesn't like the fact that these artificial products have become the norm and that their use is now systematic even when there's no need: "The oenologists have managed to sell sand in the Sahara; they flood us with products that we already have in stock! Take the example of the industrial yeasts sold to start fermentation. Using them is absurd because we already have natural native yeasts on our grapes, in our cellars, which are much more representative of our terroir than some industrial junk! Why buy a lesser, more standardized version of something we have already?"[8] And he rails against the loss of ancestral knowledge. "They made them ignorant and now they push them to buy useless, expensive products. In with the professionals, out with the winemakers. That's their philosophy!,"[9] this strong-willed winemaker says vehemently.

Dominique Derain, a Burgundy winemaker who's a fan of natural wines, i.e., those made without any oenological products, also sees the modern oenologists as fearmongers who are familiar with all the risks and flaws in wine without having ever experienced any of the pleasure or emotion in it. He shares with Stéphane Derenoncourt this disgust for a profession they both think "spits on generations of wine-makers in the name of a piece of paper, a simple degree in science."[10] "I hate these people who don't even try to under-stand why we did it this way before," explains Dominique Derain. "And who dogmatically tell us: now we know how to do it. There's a kind of arrogance in modern oenology. A pretension. For me, it's almost a bad word. You dissect the elements, you cut the cells into fifteen parts, you count them, you name them, you assume . . . It's like a mechanic taking apart a car. Except cars were made by humans, not nature!"[11]

He rails against the standardization of taste, which he sees as a general trend. "Wherever you go now, whether it's Paris, New York, or Tokyo, you'll stay in identical hotels. The taste of wine is being standardized like everything else: to soothe you, make you feel safe. You'll open a bottle, you could open a hundred of them . . . You won't have any prob-lems. But you won't have any pleasure either."[12]

The oenologists talk about making wines to respond to markets, but these poetic winemakers make wine they like. "My wine isn't made to satisfy the clients' taste; it's made because its exists in this vintage, in this place. For me, wine is an art,"[13] says Dominique Derain passionately. Inspired wine instead of consumer wine, as Stéphane Derenoncourt likes to say, provoking the anger of all his critics. "The problem is that today, more and more of these so-called natural wines are penalized by the INAO because they're considered devi-ant; now, the norm is using oenological products."[14]

These wines are thus excluded from their appellation, or "downgraded" into table wines because they are thought to be unworthy of being part of their terroir. This paradox scandalizes those who try to stay as close as possible to nature. But this doesn't seem to move the head of the INAO's wine committee, Christian Paly. For him, "The AOC isn't a right but a duty. And the first duty is to observe the production standards. If these winemakers aren't happy, if they don't feel fulfilled in this framework, no one is forcing them to stay in it,"[15] he concludes belligerently.

Geneviève Teil, a researcher at INRA (National Institute for Agronomic Research) and the author of *Le vin et l'environnement* (Wine and the Environment),[16] doesn't understand this inflexibility. To her mind, the INAO's current way of functioning is problematic, particularly because the administration had to prove to the World Trade Organization that the *appellations d'origine* correspond to objective quality. "The INAO puts markers of the particular character of each wine on a card and performs a completely rigid test," this researcher says. "You can show that it matches up, but you certainly can't show that the product is good quality."[17] And she deals the death blow: "It's not because the wastebasket is emptied every day in your hotel room or because the bed is two meters square that it's a good hotel! With this standard test, they're only looking for what's identical. But wine is like art or beauty. It's not something that you can predefine. Otherwise Picasso wouldn't exist."[18]

The detractors of these wines will tell you that they're not perfect, that they're sometimes oxidized or sour.

Dominique Derain dismisses these arguments: "Have you ever seen a pretty woman who didn't have any flaws?" the winemaker says ironically. "We have our clientele. We even sell our wines at higher prices than others, so why doesn't the administration leave us alone?"[19]

Back in Bordeaux, in a store that sells oenological products, there's a sign above the door: "Filter your wines, not your profits!" The saleswoman, seated behind the counter, seems just a little depressed. "There are lots of products, huh? Lucky we don't look too close at what's on the labels of all those boxes, otherwise we wouldn't drink wine anymore!"

In fact, why isn't there a list of ingredients on wine labels? All the additives are now listed on food products. But not on wine! Once again, Pascal Chatonnet, the head of Excell research laboratory, tells it like it is: "If we list the ingredients in containers of pigs' feet, why not do it on wine?" And he laughs: "Definitely, if we made winemakers provide a list of everything that's in their wines, some of them would have to drastically limit the oenological additives they're using! I don't see how they could do it otherwise. Their label would never be big enough!"[20]

25

MY KINGDOM FOR A CHIP

He's a tall, very thin man who looks like he stepped out of another time. He has an old-fashioned elegance with a whiff of mothballs. His hair is dyed jet-black but fades into red at his temples, like so many gentlemen who won't accept their age. He's polite but anxious. He knows that his job is always looked at with suspicion. Jean-Luc Moro sells oenological products, in fact. Of all kinds, all shapes, all brands, all types of packaging. But he's most proud of his line of oak chips. The technician is pleased that 2013 was a great year for this unrivaled product. "It's a perfect camouflage for these thin wines attacked by botrytis. It gives roundness to juices that are a bit too acidic and not ripe enough."[1]

While sales of wood chips are a hit in bad years, they also function wonderfully in the good ones. He's thrilled with how lucrative this business is. "You must admit," he purrs, "that since they were authorized by the European Commission in 2006,[2] there have only been good years for chips!"[3]

And he boasts of the merits of these few millimeters of wood that soak in the vats and let you flavor the wines as you like. But he can go on and on about their subtle nuances and differences in taste. "There are the toasted, the nontoasted."[4]

"Wine with wood is always better than wine without wood: that's the basics," scientist Jean-Philippe Fort says enthusiastically. "It's a spice! Too much kills the product, but without enough, it's not as good."[5]

But be careful: you don't use wood chips on a whim. No, this is a commitment to taste. "You don't cut down forests for fun," storms Jean-Philippe Fort, putting on his environmentalist's hat. "We simply realized that oak has a very positive effect on the quality of good as well as bad wines."[6]

Of course, there's wood and then there's wood. Barrels and chips. Oak barrels are a luxury. It's a fashion that dates from only thirty years ago at most. "At that time, people realized that to make fine wines, you needed nice clothing, that is, these new barrels,"[7] claims Jean-Philippe Fort. Alas, not everyone can afford these luxurious containers because they're so expensive. "With Valandraud, our *premier grand cru classé*, we are the biggest buyers on the right bank," Jean-Luc Thunevin explains. "Not that we're the richest, but our clients are used to our wine having the taste of luxury barrels. A taste that has evolved over the years and is much lighter and more elegant today than it was yesterday. What's our budget for this? Three hundred thousand euros a year."[8]

Consumers' palates have gradually grown accustomed to the woody taste. Especially because of the surge of wines on the French market that were created by new world

oenologists. They didn't ask all the "metaphysical" questions, to use Jean-Philippe Fort's expression, that the French
might have asked themselves at the time. They just noticed
that consumers liked the round, sweet taste created by the
addition of wood. So why spend crazy amounts and infinite
time so that wine can gradually take on a woody taste? It
was better to take the bull by the horns, and the wood by
the chips, and let the wood brew directly in the vats like a
teabag in a mug of hot water. These little wines from the
other side of the world landed here with prices that brooked
no competition. At the same time Robert Parker, the most
qualified critic, became the main Bordeaux expert, and since
he happened to like woody wines, oenologists started putting them in every which way. They were eager to season
small wines with these sacrosanct chips—a magic solution
for making small wines woody. Quickly, wood chips became
the poor man's barrels.

"You can't demonize them," insists Jean-Philippe Fort.
Plus, don't say "chips" but "alternative products." Just like
we don't say "pesticides" but "phytosanitary products." It's
less scary and above all it's more chic.

"Alternative, because it's no use dreaming," lectures
Jean-Philippe Fort. "Only two to three percent of wines
consumed worldwide are from barrels. We're in the top
wines, but for wines priced between two and five euros, we
can't afford it."

And, suddenly, he sounds almost moralizing: "You
can't bury your head in the sand. Everyone can't drive a
Ferrari or eat chicken from Bresse that has run around for

months. Wood is like everything else: there are flavored yogurts and yogurts with fruit. And giving people flavored yogurt doesn't mean you're poisoning them. You can't feed the whole global population with natural things. We have to stop fantasizing!"[9]

Basically, barrels are for rich people and chips are for everyone else. And whether we like it or not, oenologists are determined to leave poetry to the poets and simply make what they call with their usual tact "market wines."

The winemaker's touch is ancient history—hello to the wonderful era of alternative products! Anyone who objects is just a horrible reactionary rejecting both modernity and economic laws. "You've got to accept it! Why reject everything altogether? Why hide? There's a market for this. We're here to make a living!"[10]

Above all, don't mix apples and oranges, for even in the world of alternative products there are important hierarchies. At the bottom of the taste scale are chiplets, two-millimeter things in sacks that steep in the wine to flavor it rapidly. At the top of the scale are staves, wooden planks that are supposed to stay in the vats longer. The longer you infuse, the more chance there is that the woody taste will stick. Basically, chips work, but not for long. And that's why they cost less.

"Chips are great," Stéphane Derenoncourt adds with a touch of irony. "They're a knockout, like a woman with a lot of makeup on. But only in the morning, because at the end of the day, they're usually not nearly as good."[11]

Dominique Derain, the Burgundy farmer who is hesitant about the excesses of modernity, also doesn't approve of this recent trend. He knows this world well, however, because he was a cooper in his first life. Thus he finds it amusing to hear young sommeliers today tell him, just a bit dogmatically, that the taste of such and such a Burgundy appellation is oak. "This oak thing isn't over thirty years old. Before 1975, we didn't use oak barrels in Burgundy, but chestnut!" And he remembers nostalgically that when he made barrels, he put hot water inside to "draw out the bad tannins," basically, getting rid of the wood taste. "It's heresy: people forget about the wine and the woodiness takes over. I prefer the taste of wine to the taste of wood. But to each his own."[12]

Derain tells an amusing story of a sake tasting in Beaune. He saw the intelligentsia of the most prestigious Burgundy appellations there, including a well-known winemaker who was a fan of the woody taste. "He comes to talk to me and says, 'It's funny, in the sake, you can really taste the oak.' I said, 'Yes, just like wine!'"[13]

Apparently when you love it, you don't even taste this marvelous additive anymore.

Afterword

And now the gates of the kingdom close on a little world that's as cruel as it is elegant and as ferocious as it is refined. But the milieu's machinations shouldn't eclipse the spirit of the place and many winemakers' wonderful dedication to their craft.

The way they suffered in the cruel year of 2013—with rain on the flowers, hail on the new fruit, and miserable harvests—shows these men's visceral attachment to their wine, and how they're called to devote their lives to *grands crus classés*. For behind the majestic color, the cashmere texture, and the supple tannins are long hours of labor. It wouldn't take much for this marvelous principality to become a paradise. And then this wine empire would finally fall in line with the laws of the Republic and could claim to follow ethical principles.

A few commonsense reforms wouldn't cost the taxpayers a penny. The first one would be to restore the respectability of the puppet watchdog, the INAO. This institution that is supposed to maintain the quality and honor of our French terroirs is a marvelous idea. But in the hands of a few, it makes its laws in the vineyards, or, in fact, follows the principle that "might makes right" and pitilessly inflicts this dictum on the weakest. Why not end the constant conflicts of interest of this quasipublic service and finally reestablish the independence it deserves?

Plus, how is it possible that when we are so concerned with the environment and so risk averse, wine can enjoy such impunity regarding pesticides and ignore the rules that regulate all other foods? This divine nectar would come out ahead if it stated the oenological and phytosanitary products used in its production. And who knows: maybe engaging in precise labeling and a bit more transparency would make our winemakers not want to use them.

Perhaps then the French wine industry and its talented leaders could finally stand together to resist standardized taste and defend our dear terroirs. The very ones that made us great in the first place.

Acknowledgments

I'd like to thank all those who opened the door to this principality for me, who introduced me to the court, and helped me decipher the habits and customs of this inner circle. Without them, I would have been stuck at the border of this kingdom. These outsiders, who became men and women of the milieu, haven't forgotten the difficulty of joining it and have maintained a wry perspective on this enchanted fiefdom. I'm thinking especially of the consultant Stéphane Derenoncourt, the strict, strong-willed northerner, and of Saint-Émilion's bad boy, Jean-Luc Thunevin, and his wife, Murielle Andraud. Their perspective was precious.

Then there are those who, while at first reluctant, let themselves be tempted by the adventure. And who are a bit worried today, wondering about the treatment they will get. This is the case of Michel Rolland, the wine guru who was burned by Jonathan Nossiter's film *Mondovino*, the consultant Jean-Philippe Fort, Pierre Lurton, the head of

Yquem and Cheval Blanc, the witty aristocrat Stephan von Neipperg, and the critics James Suckling and Jean-Marc Quarin.

There are also those who answered my call enthusiastically, such as Hubert de Boüard and Alain Raynaud, and now seem to regret it a bit.

Plus, there are all those I can't mention because they made me promise to shield their identities, but who revealed to me the inner workings of the milieu and who, like unflappable watchdogs, prefer to stay in the shadows and continue their work.

There are those who dared to break the code of silence and reveal the plain truth of the hidden customs of the inner circle, such as Dominique Techer, the farmer–winemaker on the Pomerol plateau, Pascal Chatonnet, the head of Excell research laboratory, and Dominique Derain, the Burgundy winemaker.

There are all those who are battling in their regions and shared their experience and their knowledge of these cases: Pierre Carle and his daughter Lucile, Hubert Boidron, Sylvie Giraud, Aline Guichard.

Finally, thanks to my editor, Alexandre Wickham, who made me understand how crucial it was to bring elegance to strong and sometimes aggressive reasoning.

And, finally, thanks to all those who were willing to answer my e-mails.

To all, a big thank-you.

NOTES

Chapter One

1. Interview in Jonathan Nossiter's 2004 documentary *Mondovino*.

2. Interview with Bernard Pujol, June 24, 2013.

3. Interview with Bernard Pujol, September 30, 2013.

Chapter Two

1. Bon Pasteur (Pomerol), Rolland-Maillet (Saint-Émilion), and Bertineau Saint-Vincent (Lalande-de-Pomerol).

2. Interview with Michel Rolland, July 1, 2013.

3. Ibid.

4. Ibid.

5. Figures from SAFER, the Real Estate and Rural Planning Agency [Société d'aménagement foncier et d'établissement rural].

6. Interview with Alain Vauthier, September 17, 2013.

7. *Challenges* 349, June 13, 2013.

8. Interview with Stéphane Derenoncourt, March 18, 2013.

9. Ibid.

10. MACSF stands for Mutuelle d'assurance du corps de santé français (Mutual Insurance Company for French Health Care Professionals). "Banques, assurances, mutuelles: Les 'zinzins' sont fous de vin" [Banks, insurance companies, mutual insurance companies: Institutional investors are crazy about wine]. *Revue du Vin de France* 573, July–August 2013.

11. Ibid.

12. Ibid.

13. Interview with Michel Rolland, July 1, 2013.

14. Ibid.

15. Interview with Dominique Techer, July 16, 2012.

16. Interview with Dominique Techer, March 20, 2013.

17. Interview with Jean-Luc Thunevin, June 5, 2013.

18. Interview with Dominique Techer, March 20, 2013.

19. Interview with Jean-Luc Thunevin, June 5, 2013.

20. Interview with Michel Rolland, July 1, 2013.

21. Interview with Stéphane Derenoncourt, March 18, 2013.

Chapter Three

1. Interview with Gennaro Iorio, June 22, 2013.

2. Interview with Hubert de Boüard, June 22, 2013.

3. Interview with Fabrice Matysiak, June 16, 2013.

4. Interview with Gérard Margeon, September 20, 2013.

5. Ibid.

6. Ibid.

7. Ibid.

8. Ibid.

9. Interview with Hubert de Boüard, May 13, 2013.

10. Ibid.

11. Interview, October 24, 2012.

12. Interview with Stéphane Derenoncourt, March 18, 2013.

13. Portzamparc won the Chicago Athenaeum's prestigious international architecture prize in 2013.

14. Interview with Dominique Techer, March 20, 2013.

Chapter Four

1. Interview with Laurent Benoit, March 28, 2013.

2. Interview with Stéphane Derenoncourt, May 14, 2013.

3. The classification was changed in 1973 when Mouton Rothschild was promoted from a *second* to a *premier grand cru classé*.

4. Interview with Hubert de Boüard, June 10, 2013.

5. Interview with Stéphane Derenoncourt, May 14, 2013.

6. Interview with Christian Paly, November 14, 2013.

7. Ibid.

Chapter Five

1. Interview with Michel Rolland, July 1, 2013.

2. Ibid.

3. Interview with Alain Raynaud, January 23, 2013.

4. Ibid.

5. Ibid.

6. Hanna Agostini, Marie-Françoise Guichard, *Robert Parker, Anatomie d'un mythe* [Robert Parker: "Anatomy of a Myth"] (Paris: Scali, 2007).

7. Ibid.

8. Interview with Stéphane Derenoncourt, April 11, 2013.

9. Jean-François Quenin explained his choice of these two consultants in an e-mail of November 17, 2013: "I chose my consultants to continue improving the estate. Both Hubert de Boüard and

Alain Raynaud have good track records. Their expertise and, in my case, their discussions (they usually work together) are clearly very helpful. Plus, they can also both help me promote my wines (for example, a group presentation at the *en primeur* sales of all the wines Hubert de Boüard consults for)."

10. Interview with Justin Onclin, February 26, 2013.

11. Interview with Jean-Marc Quarin, January 25, 2013.

12. I attempted unsuccessfully to reach Hanna Agostini for comment several times.

13. Eric Conan, in *L'Express*, November 2, 2006.

14. Interview with Jean-Luc Thunevin, June 4, 2013.

Chapter Six

1. Interview with Jean-Luc Thunevin, September 29, 2013.

2. A few months after Joseph Capus's death, the National Committee of Appellations of Origin for Wines and Spirits became, by a decree of July 16, 1947, the National Institute of Appellations of Origin for Wines and Spirits.

3. Germain Lafforgue, *Le Vignoble Girondin* ["The Wine of Gironde"], preface and introduction by Joseph Capus (Paris: Louis Larmat, 1947), 35.

4. Interview with Marc Parcé, December 10, 2012.

5. Ibid.

6. Jean-Jacques Rousseau, *The Social Contract*, translated by Maurice Cranston (Penguin Classics, 1968), book 3, chap. 4.

7. Interview with Jean-Michel Deiss, June 26, 2012.

8. Interview with Christian Paly, November 14, 2013.

9. Interview with Hubert de Boüard, November 13, 2013.

10. Ibid.

11. Interview with Marc Parcé, October 15, 2012.

Chapter Seven

1. Interview with Michel Rolland, July 1, 2013.

2. Ibid.

3. Interview with Jean-Luc Thunevin, October 23, 2012.

4. Ibid.

5. Interview with Hubert de Boüard, May 13, 2013.

6. Interview with Jean-Luc Thunevin, March 19, 2013.

7. Interview with Michel Rolland, July 1, 2013.

8. Interview with Dominique Techer, March 20, 2013.

9. Interview with Pierre Lurton, October 4, 2013.

10. Interview with Jean-Luc Thunevin, March 29, 2013.

11. Interview with Jean-Luc Thunevin, March 19, 2013.

12. Interview with Hubert de Boüard, May 13, 2013.

13. "La Fleur de Boüard, un chai totalement renversant" [La Fleur de Boüard, an astounding cellar], *La Vigne* 244, July–August 2012: 40–41.

14. Interview with Pascal Chatonnet, March 28, 2013.

15. Interview with Laurent Benoit, June 7, 2013.

16. Interview with Jean-Luc Thunevin, June 6, 2013.

Chapter Eight

1. Interview with Alain Dourthe, February 14, 2013.

2. Interview with Alain Dourthe, March 28, 2013.

3. Interview with Pascal Chatonnet, March 28. 2013.

4. Ibid.

5. Interview with Pascal Chatonnet, February 28, 2013.

6. Interview with Pascal Chatonnet, February 15, 2013.

7. Interview with Pascal Chatonnet, February 28, 2013.

8. When I asked Magali Grinbaum of the French Wine-Making Institute about these issues, she did not reply.

9. The fungicide in question is folpet, which was originally intended to fight mildew or oidium.

10. Interview with Alain Dourthe, March 28, 2013.

11. This is the definition proposed by the World Health Organization in 2002 and quoted by ANSES, the French Agency for Food, Environmental, and Occupational Health and Safety: "A potential endocrine disruptor is an exogenous substance or mixture with properties that may alter functions of the endocrine system in an intact organism, or its progeny or (sub)populations."

12. Interview with Pascal Chatonnet, February 28, 2013.

13. Interview with Pascal Chatonnet, March 28, 2013.

14. "Pesticides in French Wine," *New York Times* editorial, January 2, 2014.

15. Jérôme Baudouin, "Pesticides, les grands vins passés au crible" [Pesticides: scrutinizing fine wines], *Revue du Vin de France* 537, December 2009–January 2010.

16. Substances broken down from folpet (an antimildew and anti-oidium fungicide) and pyrimethanil (an antibotrytis chemical that was also present in the Burgundy).

17. Jérôme Baudouin, "Vins et pesticides: sont-ils solubles dans le temps?" [Wine and pesticides: are they soluble over time?], *Revue du Vin de France* 539, March 2010.

18. An antibotrytis chemical.

19. An antibotrytis chemical.

20. Interview with Pascal Chatonnet, February 14, 2013.

21. Interview, March 28, 2013.

22. As Pascal Chatonnet explains in his research: "Carbendazim is an active substance that is not allowed to be sold in France. However, the European MRL for carbendazim on wine grapes is

.5 mg/kg. The regulations allow carbendazim to be in wine even though its use is banned." Presentation, February 14, 2013.

23. Interview with Pascal Chatonnet, February 14, 2013.

24. When I contacted Mouton Cadet, the company responded in an e-mail of December 13, 2013, from Adrien Laurent. He emphasized that "UFC Que Choisir has a very questionable interpretation of the results of its study" and spoke of "alarmist conclusions." "Presenting the results as 'amount of residues'" makes, according to him, "no sense given that each product has different characteristics." He adds that it is not "rational to compare the 'amount of residues' to the standards for drinking water (presented as the base drink) because water is simply not in contact with treatment products." Moreover, "the presence of trace amounts of 14 substances in Mouton Cadet is connected to the variety of [their] suppliers. Mouton Cadet comes from a rigorous selection of the best parcels of various Bordeaux terroirs." Finally, he adopts a reassuring tone: "The quantities of residues detected in Mouton Cadet present no risk to the consumer . . . As a reminder, to reach what is called the daily allowed dose (DAD), a typical man would have to drink several dozen liters of wine every day throughout his life." Laurent adds that "Mouton Cadet, since its establishment in 1930, has become the number one Bordeaux wine sold worldwide. Its presence in 150 countries is the best proof of its quality and its compliance with the most diverse and drastic regulations."

25. The owner declined to respond to my questions.

26. UFC Que Choisir emphasizes that "five Bordeaux wines took the prize" for the highest levels of residues in wine. No. 518, October 2013.

27. Interview with Hervé Jestin, July 12, 2012.

Chapter Nine

1. Interview with Dominique Techer, May 15, 2013.

2. Ibid.

3. Ibid.

4. with Stéphane Derenoncourt, May 14, 2013.

5. Interview with Dominique T Interview echer, May 15, 2013.

Chapter Ten

1. Interview with Jean-Luc Thunevin, April 10, 2013.

2. Interview with Pascal Chatonnet, March 28, 2013.

3. Interview with Jean-Marc Quarin, January 25, 2013.

4. Interview with Pascal Chatonnet, March 28, 2013.

5. Interview with Jean-Luc Thunevin, April 11, 2013.

6. Interview with Pierre Lurton, June 22, 2013.

7. Interview with Franck Dubourdieu, January 25, 2013.

8. Interview with Jean-Luc Thunevin, March 29, 2013.

9. Ibid.

10. Interview with Jean-Luc Thunevin, March 29, 2013.

11. Interview with Jean-Luc Thunevin, March 29, 2013.

12. Interview with Dominique Techer, March 20, 2013.

13. Interview with Jean-Luc Thunevin, June 5, 2013.

Chapter Eleven

1. Interview with Jean-Philippe Fort, March 20, 2013.

2. Ibid.

3. Ibid.

4. Adam Lechmere, "Bordeaux Winemakers Give Their Take on Derenoncourt's 'Special' *en Primeur* Samples," *Decanter*, May 20, 2013.

5. Interview with Dominique Techer, March 20, 2013.

6. Ibid.

7. Interview with Jean-Luc Thunevin, April 10, 2013.

8. Interview with Gérard Margeon, September 20, 2013.

9. Ibid.

Chapter Twelve

1. Interview with Stephan von Neipperg, May 30, 2013.

2. Interview with Stéphane Derenoncourt, May 14, 2013.

3. Interview with Stephan von Neipperg, May 30, 2013.

4. Interview with Wei Xu, May 20, 2013.

5. Gilles Berdin, *Autour d'une bouteille, avec Murielle Andraud et Jean-Luc Thunevin* ["Opening a Bottle with Murielle Andraud and Jean-Luc Thunevin"] (Bordeaux: Elytis, 2013), 121.

6. Interview with Wei Xu, May 20, 2013.

7. Ibid.

8. Ibid.

9. Interview with Nelly Blau-Picard, May 20, 2013.

Chapter Thirteen

1. Figures from the Vinea Transaction network.

2. Interview with Hubert de Boüard, June 10, 2013.

3. Interview with Stéphane Derenoncourt, May 14, 2013.

4. Interview with Peter Kwok, August 24, 2013.

5. Ibid.

6. 2012 *en primeur* sales.

7. Interview with Peter Kwok, October 6, 2013.

8. Interview with Peter Kwok, August 24, 2013.

9. Tracfin 2012 Annual Analysis and Activity Report. Tracfin stands for Traitement du Renseignement et Action Contre les Circuits

Financiers Clandestins [Information and Action Against Illegal Financial Transactions].

10. E-mail from Dominique Techer, August 3, 2013.

11. Interview with Stéphane Derenoncourt, May 14, 2013.

Chapter Fourteen

1. Interview with Aline Guichard-Goldschmidt, October 18, 2012.

2. Interview with Dominique Techer, November 27, 2012.

3. Interview with Aline Guichard-Goldschmidt, October 18, 2012.

4. Ibid.

5. Interview with Aline Guichard-Goldschmidt, October 22, 2012.

6. Ibid.

7. E-mail from Christian Moueix, November 18, 2013.

8. In the same e-mail of November 18, 2013, Christian Moueix commented on his position as follows: "I greatly admired Olivier Guichard. His business relations with my father and with me were extremely courteous. Our trust was reciprocal. Recently, we recommended a young vineyard manager to alleviate his concerns. At that time we handled sales for his three châteaux: Châteaux Siaurac, Lalande-de-Pomerol; Château Vray Croix de Gay, Pomerol; and Château Le Prieuré, Saint-Émilion *grand cru classé*.

"After his death, we naturally continued relations with his heirs, Aline Guichard and especially Paul Goldschmidt. They wanted to take over sales in France, which we understood and agreed to.

"On the other hand, once the exclusive export rights were questioned, a break became unavoidable. This was a great loss for the Jean-Pierre Moueix company."

9. Interview with Aline Guichard-Goldschmidt, October 22, 2012.

10. Interview with Aline Guichard-Goldschmidt, October 18, 2012.

11. Ibid.

12. Ibid.

Chapter Fifteen

1. Jean-Marie Garde, president of the wine syndicate, explained in an e-mail of November 21, 2013: "For the syndicate, it was never an issue of 'exiles,' since all the winemakers producing on the Pomerol AOC are members of the syndicate recognized as a DMO (defense and management organization)."

2. Press release by the exiles and interview with Aline Guichard of November 27, 2012.

3. Council of State, no. 334575, March 9, 2012.

4. This is the reply I received from Mr. Jean-Marie Garde, president of the Pomerol syndicate, in an e-mail of November 21, 2013: "The Pomerol AOC extends over the entirety of the town of Pomerol and part of that of Libourne; approximately 30% of Pomerol wines are in Libourne. The proximity zone was opened to the whole of the town of Libourne because it is an administrative unit, in keeping with European regulations."

5. Interview with Christian Paly, November 14, 2013.

6. Ibid.

7. E-mail of November 21, 2013, from Mr. Bruno de Lambert, vice president of the Pomerol syndicate: "Concerning the personal attack against me, I will merely reply that the situation of the Château de Sales and its legal entity follow a court decision of December 28, 1928 [in fact, the official quality charter of the appellation reads December 29], a decision confirmed by the decree of 1936 and thus in the quality charter; I should also specify that these wines have always been made in the Pomerol AOC."

8. César Compadre, "À Pomerol, l'hippodrome laisse place à la vigne" [In Pomerol, the racetrack gives way to vineyards], *Sud-Ouest*, April 22, 2011.

9. Jean-Louis Trocard's e-mail of November 20, 2013, adds more details: "OK, this means that I still support my colleagues on the substance of the issue.

"As you correctly pointed out, Benoît has had the possibility to expand onto the racetrack, so we are going to produce a new wine that will be called Château Porte Chic. So we are cultivating 3.5 hectares in Pomerol with two vintages and we decided that this was the minimum for investing in a cellar . . .

"So there has been a change in strategy that led me to decide not to continue the lawsuit with my colleagues."

10. Interview with Christian Paly, November 14, 2013.

11. E-mail of November 21, 2013, from the president of the Pomerol syndicate, Jean-Marie Garde: "It was never a question of exclusion. If the Council of State recognizes the current quality charter, the winemakers who currently make their wine outside the AOC will not be excluded, as they have until 2021 to conform to the quality charter. To do so, they will not have to pull out a single grapevine, as the concerned properties have buildings that can be converted or they can rent cellars currently available in the Pomerol AOC."

12. Letter from Christian Moueix to Guichard family, December 15, 2011.

13. E-mail from Christian Moueix to author, November 18, 2013.

14. "May your writings contribute to peace in the Pomerol appellation." Ibid.

15. Council of State, decision of December 17, 2013.

16. The Council of State questioned the several reorganizations of the proximity zone. But that didn't stop the wine lords, who always have a backup plan. They decided to get by without it and to require a stricter reading of the quality charter, slamming the small wine producers in Pomerol once again.

Chapter Sixteen

1. General Winemakers' Syndicate, *La Champagne Viticole* [The Champagne Wine Region] 762, November 2010.

2. Interview with Bertrand Auboyneau, February 17, 2012.

3. Interview with Bertrand Auboyneau, April 12, 2012.

4. Interview with Jean-Sébastien Fleury, June 12, 2012.

5. E-mail to author, October 12, 2012.

6. Interview, October 19, 2012.

7. Interview, November 14, 2013.

8. Ibid.

9. Ibid.

10. Interview with Bertrand Gautherot, July 10, 2012.

11. Ibid.

12. Ibid.

13. E-mail from Joachim Beaufort to author, July 12, 2012.

14. Ibid.

15. Interview with Quentin Beaufort, July 11.

16. Paul-François Vranken did not reply to an e-mail of November 6, 2013.

17. Semiannual fiscal report of June 30, 2012.

18. *Challenges*, July 20, 2011. He is number thirty-six in the same magazine's 2013 list of the top fifty wine fortunes, with a net worth of €200 million.

19. Interview with Julienne Guihard, December 4, 2012.

20. Philippe Feneuil did not reply to an e-mail of November 6, 2013.

21. Interview with Julienne Guihard, December 4, 2012.

22. Julienne Guihard, "Scandale au SGV: Trois millions dans la nature" [Scandal at the SGV: The vanishing three million]," *L'Union*, December 16, 2009.

23. Interview with a Champagne syndicate member, October 14, 2012.

24. Interview with a Champagne syndicate member, October 19, 2012.

25. Julienne Guihard, "Scandale au SGV: Trois millions dans la nature" [Scandal at the SGV: The vanishing three million]," *L'Union*, December 16, 2009.

26. Ibid.

27. Attempts to reach Rolland Chaillon by phone, by e-mail on November 6, 2013, and by letter on November 6, 2013, were unsuccessful.

28. Interview with Julienne Guichard, December 4, 2012.

29. Ibid.

30. Civil parties must pay fees to bring criminal charges.

31. Judge Craighero did not reply to my letter of November 6, 2013.

32. Minutes of the national division of financial investigations of Nanterre published by *L'Union* on February 24, 2011.

33. Ibid.

34. "Procès en diffamation intenté par Franken et Feneuil" [Libel suit filed by Vranken and Feneuil], *L'Union-L'Ardennais*, January 23, 2012.

35. *Les Échos* 18627, April 3, 2002.

Chapter Seventeen

1. Interview with Jacques Beaufort, July 4, 2012.

2. Ibid.

3. Bulletin d'Informations Phytosanitaires de la Direction Régionale de l'Alimentation, de l'Agriculture et de la Forêt de Champagne-Ardenne [Pesticide News Report of the Regional Office of Food, Agriculture, and Forests of Champagne-Ardenne] 32, July 2012.

4. Thierry Dromard, *Le Journal de Saône-et-Loire*, June 10, 2013.

5. It has become the Research Institute on Science and Technology for the Environment and Agriculture, or IRSTEA [Institut de recherche en sciences et technologies pour l'environnement et l'agriculture].

6. *Pesticides, agriculture et environnement: Réduire l'utilisation des pesticides et en limiter les impacts environnementaux* [Pesticides, agriculture, and the environment: Reducing the use of pesticides and limiting their environmental impact], collective authorship. Report of the assessment by INRA and CEMAGREF at the request of the Ministry of Agriculture and Fishing and the Ministry of Ecology and Sustainable Development, December 2005, 44.

7. O. Viret, W. Siegfried, E. Holliger, U. Rausigl, "Comparison of Spray Deposits and Efficiency Against Powdery Mildew of Aerial and Ground-Based Spraying Equipment in Viticulture," *Crop Protection* 22 (2003): 1023–32.

8. Ibid., 18: "Among the banned active substances, lindane was found on all the sites. Methyl parathion, tebutam, atrazine, and norflurazon were only detected on certain sites."

9. Florence Coignard, Christine Lorente, Département santé environnement [Department of Health and the Environment], *Exposition aérienne aux pesticides des populations à proximité des zones agricoles. Bilan et perspectives du Programme Régional Intercire* [Aerial exposure to pesticides of populations near agricultural areas. Summary and perspectives of the Intercire Regional Program], Institut de veille Sanitaire [Institute of Health Monitoring] (2006), 18.

10. Toxicological record established by the technical and medical departments of INRS (National Institute of Research and Security), with the participation of ANSES, 2011 edition.

11. Up to $1{,}242 \text{mg/m}^3$.

12. Florence Coignard, Christine Lorente, *Exposition aérienne* . . . ., 17: "Mancozeb, which is very frequently used, could not be identified for reasons of analytical feasibility."

13. As indicated in a 2005 report cowritten by AFSSE (the French Agency for Environmental Health and Safety) and INERIS (the National Institute for the Industrial Environment and Risk): "L'épandage aérien de produits antiparasitaires [Aerial Spraying of Pesticide Products]. Report of the institutional working group in charge of AFSSE's jurisdiction, June 2005, 78.

14. *La Vigne* 243, June 2012.

15. Ibid.

16. Ibid., 22.

17. "Bulletin d'informations phytosanitaires de la Direction Régionale de l'Alimentation, de l'Agriculture et de la Forêt de Champagne-Ardenne" [Pesticide News Report of the Regional Office of Food, Agriculture, and Forests in Champagne-Ardenne], no. 32.

18. Interview with a winemaker, July 10, 2012.

19. Interview with a vineyard worker in Aube, July 10, 2012.

20. Le Monde.fr with AFP, August 22, 2012.

Chapter Eighteen

1. Dominique Techer, "Intervention divine à Saint-Émilion" [Divine intervention in Saint-Émilion], vindicateur.fr.

2. "Le classement de Saint-Émilion: Le recul du terroir" [The Saint-Émilion classification: The decline of terroir], article written on January 29, 2013, and published in *Vitisphère*.

3. Ibid.

4. Ibid.

5. Interview with Saint-Émilion château owner, January 10, 2013.

6. Interview with Jean-Luc Thunevin, October 23, 2012.

7. Jean-François Arnaud, *Challenges* 349, June 13, 2013.

8. Jean-Marc Quarin, *Chronicle* 154, September 1, 2013.

9. Ibid.

10. Ibid.

11. Ibid.

12. Interview with Pierre Carle, June 18, 2013.

13. Interview with a winemaker, October 2, 2012.

14. Interview with Dominique Techer, August 7, 2012.

15. Troplong Mondot had become a *premier grand cru classé* in the 2006 classification. This classification was later suspended by the courts. Some declassified châteaux had questioned its legitimacy and started a legal battle. After many legal twists and turns, the French parliament ended up resolving the issue in article 65 of the law on simplification and clarification of laws and streamlining of procedures of May 12, 2009. Those who had attained classified status were allowed to keep it, and those who were declassified could retain their previous classification until the establishment of the 2012 classification.

Chapter Nineteen

1. Interview with Marie-Lys Bibeyran, June 20, 2013.

2. Ibid.

3. Ibid.

4. Ibid.

5. Ibid.

6. Ibid.

7. Ibid.

8. Ibid.

9. Ibid.

10. Ibid.

11. Ibid.

12. Ibid.

13. Ibid.

14. Ibid.

15. Ibid.

Chapter Twenty

1. Interview with Dominique Techer, July 16, 2012.

2. Ibid.

3. Interview with Pierre Carle, September 19, 2012.

4. Croque-Michotte was declassified in 1996, but since Pierre Carle had just taken over the management of the château, he didn't dare challenge this decision at that time. He put his energies into regaining classification in 2006.

5. Château Troplong Mondot; Château Bellefont-Belcier; Château Destieux; Château Fleur Cardinale; Château Grand Corbin; Château Grand Corbin-Despagne; Château Pavie-Macquin; Château Monbousquet.

6. Upon several third-party objections from vineyards that were classified by the decree of December 12, 2006, the Bordeaux administrative court upheld its position in a decision of October 28, 2008. On March 12, 2009, the Bordeaux administrative appeals court upheld the decision of the Bordeaux administrative court of July 1, 2008, which nullified the 2006 Saint-Émilion classification, and the decision of the Bordeaux administrative court of October 28, 2008, which rejected third-party objections from several vineyards challenging the decision of July 1, 2008.

7. Interview with Pierre Carle, September 19, 2012.

8. Château Troplong Mondot and Château Destieux.

9. Law no. 2008-776 of August 4, 2008.

10. Article 65 of the law on simplification and clarification of laws and streamlining of procedures, no. 2009-526.

11. Sixty-eight applications at €6,000 and twenty-eight applications at €7,500 for a total of €618,000.

12. An e-mail of November 18, 2013, to Mr. Philippe Castéja received no reply.

13. Hubert de Boüard was present on November 16, 2010, June 16, 2011, and April 10, 2012. Philippe Castéja missed only the meeting of June 16, 2011.

14. Interview with François de Contencin, May 2, 2013.

15. Minutes of the Saint-Émilion Wine Council board of directors meeting of May 21, 2013.

16. Asked about this issue, its president, Jean-François Quenin, responded in an e-mail of November 17, 2013: "The Saint-Émilion classification is above all a collective benefit. In particular, it allows:

- to offer a segmentation of wines and thereby inform the consumer,
- to promote Saint-Émilion appellation wines (classification is a sign of quality),
- to encourage the vineyards who want to apply for classification in the pursuit of excellence.

It is therefore logical that the Wine Council defend it (supporting the ministry and INAO)."

17. Minutes of the Saint-Émilion Wine Council board of directors meeting of May 21, 2013.

18. Ibid.

19. Interview with François de Contencin, June 18, 2013.

Chapter Twenty-one

1. Translator's added footnote: translation Norman R. Shapiro, *The Complete Fables of Jean de la Fontaine* (Champaign: University of Illinois Press, 2007).

2. Interview with Hubert de Boüard, May 13, 2013.

3. Interview with Pierre-Olivier Clouet, October 18, 2013.

4. The Rohan family motto was: "King, I cannot be, Duke, deign not to be, Rohan am I."

5. Interview with Jean-Luc Thunevin, September 17, 2013.

Chapter Twenty-two

1. Interview, April 10, 2013.

2. Ibid.

3. Interview, April 10, 2013.

4. Ibid.

5. Ibid.

6. Ibid.

7. November 22, 2012, Philippe Dova site (Aujourd'hui La Chine).

8. Interview, April 27, 2013.

9. Ibid.

10. Interview with Wei Xu, May 20, 2013.

11. Interview, April 27, 2013.

Chapter Twenty-three

1. Interview, April 9, 2013.

2. Interview with Hubert de Boüard, November 13, 2013.

3. Ibid.

4. Ibid.

Chapter Twenty-four

1. Interview, June 19, 2013.

2. Interview with Jean-Philippe Fort, October 3, 2013.

3. Ibid.

4. Interview with Dominique Techer, October 4, 2013.

5. Interview with Stéphane Derenoncourt, October 3, 2013.

6. Ibid.

7. Ibid.

8. Interview with Dominique Techer, October 4, 2013.

9. Ibid.

10. Interview, October 24, 2013.

11. Interview with Dominique Derain, May 21, 2013.

12. Ibid.

13. Ibid.

14. Interview with Dominique Techer, July 16, 2012.

15. Interview with Christian Paly, November 14, 2013.

16. Geneviève Teil, Sandrine Barrey, Pierre Floux, and Antoine Hennion, *Le vin et l'environnement* ("Wine and the Environment"), Presses des Mines, 2011.

17. Interview with Geneviève Teil, August 31, 2012.

18. Ibid.

19. Interview with Dominique Derain, May 21, 2013.

20. Interview with Pascal Chatonnet, February 28, 2013.

Chapter Twenty-five

1. Interview with Jean-Luc Moro , October 21, 2013.

2. They were authorized by European Commission regulation no. 2165/2005 of December 20, 2005.

3. Interview, October 21, 2013.

4. Ibid.

5. Interview with Jean-Philippe Fort, March 20, 2013.

6. Interview with Jean-Philippe Fort, June 19, 2013.

7. Interview with Jean-Philippe Fort, March 20, 2013.

8. Interview with Jean-Luc Thunevin, March 20, 2013.

9. Interview with Jean-Philippe Fort, June 19, 2013.

10. Ibid.

11. Interview with Stéphane Derenoncourt, October 25, 2013.

12. Interview with Dominique Derain, May 21, 2013.

13. Interview with Dominique Derain, September 13, 2012.